"Laura Dabundo's collection of essays and poems are enjoyable because they are well-observed and beautifully written. But they are also joyous, full of the discoveries of memory, of human connections and of the difficult journey to the fullness of gratitude and salvation."

—ANTHONY GROOMS
Author of *Bombingham* and *The Vain Conversation*

"Laura Dabundo's beautiful narrative—a childhood shaped by her grandmother's faith, as well as her rigorous (sometimes amusing) adherence to grammatical exactness, and an adulthood shaped by travel to Celtic spiritual sites—converges to sustain and deepen her through her later physical crises. In elegant language worthy of her grandmother, Dabundo describes her growing discernment of 'the divine light that lingers on the edge of our lives.'"

—FLEDA BROWN
Author of *Flying through a Hole in the Storm*

"A captivating example of thought and identity emerging from the writing process. Very beautiful and evocative memoir of the author's western Pennsylvania childhood, an adult pilgrimage to Ireland, and an inward journey through illness to re bringing to life of the author's grandmother, who rai hauntingly Victorian setting, is particularly beautifull

—LINDA G
Author of *Cosas: Folk Art Travels in Mexico* and *Boomer: Rai

"Reading Laura Dabundo's poems and essays is like a visit with a wise and humorous friend. She details the challenges of her unique upbringing by a singular grandmother, her personal faith journey, and the losses in her own life with searing honesty and poignant humor, finding 'thin places' between the spiritual and material realms in unexpected events. In sum, she presents a moving testimony that the trajectory of an individual life constitutes a spiritual pilgrimage."

—LINDA W. MCFADDEN
Author of *In Brigid's Footsteps: The Return of the Divine Feminine*

"This is an illuminating portrait of an extraordinary and passionate woman. She offers us not only the important difference between being reared and being raised—she was *reared* by her grandmother—but also how much richer life is when one uses language properly. Descriptions of persons and places come alive through a colorful panoply of words. Her journeys, on which the reader is given the pleasure of joining along, include reflections on the evolving role of faith and an exploration of the importance of relationships."

—BARBARA JEAN BROWN
Cofounder of Anamchara Fellowship

When the Parallel Converge

_for Glenda Hogg
a dedicated Episcopalian
and a good and
caring servant of
the community._

When the Parallel Converge

_May your pilgrimage
go well!_

_By_ LAURA DABUNDO

_Laura Dabundo
10 October 2021_

RESOURCE _Publications_ · Eugene, Oregon

WHEN THE PARALLEL CONVERGE

Copyright © 2021 Laura Dabundo. All rights reserved. Except for brief quotations in critical publications or reviews, no part of this book may be reproduced in any manner without prior written permission from the publisher. Write: Permissions, Wipf and Stock Publishers, 199 W. 8th Ave., Suite 3, Eugene, OR 97401.

Resource Publications
An Imprint of Wipf and Stock Publishers
199 W. 8th Ave., Suite 3
Eugene, OR 97401

www.wipfandstock.com

PAPERBACK ISBN: 978-1-7252-9761-6
HARDCOVER ISBN: 978-1-7252-9760-9
EBOOK ISBN: 978-1-7252-9762-3

04/09/21

Many Scriptural quotations contained herein are from the New Revised Standard Version (NRSV) Bible, copyright © 1989 by the Division of Christian Education of the National Council of the Churches of Christ in the U.S.A., and are used by permission. All rights reserved.

Some Scriptural quotations contained herein are from the Revised English Bible (REB), copyright © 1989 by Oxford University Press and Cambridge University Press and are used by permission. All rights reserved.

Two Scriptural quotations contained herein are from the TANAKH, copyright © 1985 by The Jewish Publication Society. All rights reserved.

Some Scriptural quotations contained herein are from The Bible, the Authorized King James Version (KJV) with Apocrypha. Published by Oxford University Press. All rights reserved.

For grandchildren of Marjorie and Harry Raab

Connie and Harry Raab;
Fritz, Sibyl, David, and Eric Seachrist;
Cynthie Morgenthaler; and Marjie Walsh

May I arrive at every place,

may I return home;

may the way in which I spend be a way without loss.

"THE PATH I WALK" (CELTIC DEVOTIONAL TEXT)
CELTIC SPIRITUALITY (TRANSLATED BY OLIVER DAVIES)

Contents

Acknowledgments

IT IS MY PRIVILEGE to extend my gratitude to Linda Jordan Tucker and Janice Goodfellow Carter, again, ever careful readers, advisors, and editors. I would like also to thank my cousins Cynthie Morgenthaler, Harry Raab, David Seachrist, and Marjie Walsh, who read an earlier, mostly completed version of the first chapter and offered very helpful suggestions and corrections. My spiritual director, the Rev. Michael Stuchbery of the Anglican Church of Canada, was of immense benefit to my work on the third chapter, for which I am grateful.

It is also my pleasure to recognize *Share, Literary and Art Magazine* for permission to publish "Pilgrim, Tread Softly, for This is Hallowed Ground" and also *Flycatcher Magazine* for permission to publish "Welsh Waters."

It is proper as well to thank my cousin Marjie Walsh for sharing the letter her mother received from our grandmother and allowing me to include it here.

Last, many may will notice that while there are identifiable names in Chapter 1, in Chapters 2 and 3, names are withheld. This was deliberate. I did not want to omit anyone, but also I did not feel that it was my right to single anyone out or to exclude inadvertently anyone. I kept a fairly accurate list while I was recuperating, but it could well be incomplete. Legion were those who looked out for me, including physicians, nurses, aides, clergy, family, and friends. Please know that their names are all inscribed in my heart with my unending gratitude and prayers that their good deeds and works are recorded in the divine Book of Life.

Abbreviations

BCP	The Book of Common Prayer Together with the Psalter of Psalms of David, 1986
KJV	The Bible, The Authorized King James Version
NRSV	The Holy Bible, The New Revised Standard Version
REB	The Revised English Bible
TANAKH	TANAKH, A New Translation of The Holy Scriptures According to the Traditional Hebrew Text

Introduction

As a title, the phrase "when the parallel converge" came to me with great impetus during an otherwise uninspiring geometry class in junior high school. I was taken with the concept that parallel lines, no matter how closely they are positioned, never meet. It seemed to me that there must be a place at which they did intersect or even merge. I decided then and there that that would be my title for a book. And many unwritten or unfinished stories resulted, but the title always was an allure. I cannot put into words how it spoke to me, but to what it pointed fascinated me nonetheless. Then, half dozen or so years later in an art history class in college, the vanishing point toward which all parallel lines tend in two-dimensional paintings seized my imagination anew. This is what I sought, a paradox that both never ends yet also disappears, dissipates, dissolves, like the Cheshire cat, perhaps, and still also is that to which all things incline. My journey to write about this paradox has continued unabated and lifelong.

Some have questioned the form of the title, noting that grammatically either "Parallel" or "Converge" ought to have an "s" at the end. Thus, the title by that reasoning should be, correctly, "When the Parallels Converge" or "When the Parallel Converges." I have reflected on these possibilities, but the original phrasing is how I have always heard the title in my head. On the one hand, this original form functions conditionally, as in the subjunctive, emphasizing the ambiguous "when" such as whenever, if ever, if now, in some eternal now, or yet to come. On the other hand, there is an elision between those two words, which the mind of the reader or contemplator may replace as the spirit lists. The missing word might be "times," "emotions," "moods," or other capacities or categories as I delineate shortly. I hope the reader agrees.

A pilgrimage is, of course, a journey toward a special destination. Conventionally, the term includes the arrival at the destination as the denouement of the trip. However, as T. S. Eliot has written, a spiritual pilgrimage is a circular movement, like the arc of the Christian Bible, which begins in the Garden of Eden and ends in the New Jerusalem, the garden reborn, reconfigured, redeemed, as Northrop Frye has argued. Perhaps, the point of spiritual pilgrimage is the coming home yet to a home transformed. And what about the vanishing point? What has vanished? The pilgrimage? The travel? Its travails? Its testings? Perhaps on the surface, this is true, but underneath or beyond and within something, some place, someone has been transformed.

The first offering in this collection, "Many Waters Cannot Quench Love," is an attempt to remember and to share the most extraordinary woman I have ever known, my widowed maternal grandmother Marjorie Eleanor Stiff Raab (8 March 1900 to 26 June 1991), as old as the years, her younger daughter used to say. My grandmother took me into her home in Johnstown, Pennsylvania, and brought me up from the time I was 14 months old, when my mother died as a result of polio. My father in south Jersey could most likely have found a way to manage, but this seemed the better arrangement in the early 1950s. My grandmother gave up her newly discovered career as a high-school English teacher, begun after World War II when her husband suddenly died. She was independent, bright, witty, principled, kind, devout, and grieving as long as I knew her. The essay addresses what she gave me and modeled as a life of Christian service and devotion. The source of the title is provided in the chapter. The definitive resource on Johnstown's catastrophe is David McCullough's *The Johnstown Flood*, and a more recent narrative can be found in Al Roker's *Ruthless Tide: the Heroes and Villains of the Johnstown Flood, America's Astonishing Gilded Age Disaster*. Also, Robert Jeschonek wrote a charming book about Johnstown's premier department store called *Penn Traffic Forever*.

The final part of this section is a letter that my cousin Marjie Walsh serendipitously found in an old cookbook of her mother's while this manuscript was being copyedited. She asked me to explain some of the references, and with her permission I include it here for the reader to hear Marjorie Raab in her own voice, with spelling and punctuation unchanged and written in our grandmother's elegant, graceful, most legible, and familiar script. My additions or clarifications are in brackets. The letter is inside a card that features a recipe for "rum cream pie" from a restaurant in Williamsburg.

The letter raises several issues relevant to the contents of this chapter, but preeminently what it shows is the centrality for her of her family, beyond all else. Then, specifically in connection with this memoir, other matters arise. For one, both the card and part of the discussion pertain to my grandmother's vexed relationship with cooking. She was drawn to the culinary arts yet also is subtly conveying an apprehension that she is obligated to the mother of a childhood friend of mine for feeding and entertaining me multiple times, not something she felt adequate to recompense. Also, one hears here my grandmother's enchantment with proper and civil language. Third, her particular interest in seeing *The Lion in Winter* no doubt stemmed from her admiration for Katherine Hepburn, an alumna of Bryn Mawr, of one of the Seven Sisters like herself.

Fourth, the letter addresses the importance of the church to my grandmother and to guiding me into participation in its activities. Along with that comes the final paragraph about her illness, which characteristically humbly she saves till the very end, although that might well have been by what my aunt would have been most affected. I am fairly certain that I recall this incident. My grandmother awoke in the night feeling ill, as she describes, and awakened me to call her physician, who came at once. He gave her some medicine and instructions, and she recovered. Later, we told the new priest mentioned in the letter about that night (the Rev. Andrew Parker Bateman Allis, now deceased). He said that we could have called him to come to our house in the night. My grandmother thanked him and told me later when I asked that she would have liked that.

One last aspect of the letter that I can clarify is the séance. As the chapter shows, my grandmother was curious about spiritualism. I have no doubt that it was under her influence that I might have suggested we try to conjure Vachel Lindsay, surely a curious subject for high-school girls to fancy. However, he was a poet whom my grandmother encouraged me to read and to study because she had seen him recite at a poetry reading in Johnstown in the early 1900s.

The next three works, two poems and one prose piece, all treat in different ways my participation in Celtic pilgrimages to places in the British Isles and Ireland, which share a Celtic heritage. Before Christianity came to that part of the world, the Celts reigned and worshiped in pagan splendor. Christianity then and there, unlike elsewhere, adapted to rather than stifled native customs and traditions. Thus, Celtic Christianity emerged and still has much to teach us today. Traveling to these places, as I have done and record here, on trips organized and guided by religious leaders, means visiting sites associated with the Celts, including ruins, landscapes, extant formations, all still imbued with a sense of the living connection of the natural and human, animate and inanimate, the here and now with what has been and what will be, the physical and spiritual. These locations and scenes are peaceful when not overrun by tourists and bespeak transcendence within immanence, grace and joy.

These trips have become important lodestars in my spiritual development, my larger pilgrimage of life. Anyone in search of fairly recent, excellent resources on Celtic Christianity might consult works by Esther de Waal, Timothy Joyce, J. Philip Newell, John O'Donohue, Herbert O'Driscoll, Edward Sellner, and Ray Simpson among many others. To begin, here are two poems, "Pilgrim, Tread Softly, for this is Hallowed Ground" and "Welsh Waters," written in response to Celtic pilgrimages, the first in Ireland and the second in Wales. "Welsh Waters" is a serendipitous title in this book because it might also refer to the Johnstown Flood inasmuch as Cambria County, in which Johnstown is found, bears the Latin name for Wales.

The next piece of the book and the third part of this sequence, "Celtic Travels," is "Thin Space," a dark night of the soul that encompassed me when a delayed flight home from an Irish pilgrimage landed me overnight on a holiday weekend when not a hotel room was to be found in the environs of the North Jersey airport. I was alone among a crowd in a phantasmagoric, surreal ordeal. The title is a Celtic term defined in several places here as my pilgrimage unfolds.

The last two parts constitute "Infirmities." "Let This Mortal Flesh Be Silent" and "My Eventful Year: A Healing Journal" focus initially on the mortal, physical self. The penultimate piece of the collection and the first item here is a poem about an attack of shingles that afflicted me when I was in England at the very end of a Scots/English Celtic pilgrimage. Though I went to a British medical facility and was thereby medicated to some extent, I flew home the next day with one eye swollen shut and immediately went to an Emergency Room. My British medicine was not strong or soon enough, it seemed, and I was in danger of losing my vision in one eye. But I did not, but not before I suffered post-herpetic neuralgia, which is what the poem concerns, finally effectively silenced by wondrous gabapentin. The title is a slight modification of an old hymn, "Let All Mortal Flesh Keep Silence," haunting, beautiful music based on centuries-old French sources, with words from what is called "The Liturgy of St. James," synchronously the name of my parish now and at the time of the writing of this piece but yet a hymn that more often brings me back to the church of my youth and of "Many Waters Cannot Quench Love."

The last essay I wrote came from a journal I kept intermittently when, out of the blue, I came down with a staphylococcal infection in my spine and throughout my body that nearly killed me and certainly crippled me, taking away my ability to walk. Excellent medical care and physical therapy with much attentive intercessory prayer healed me. In the process, I learned about myself, my faith, my life, as I hope the prose makes manifest.

My many years of college teaching the Hebrew Scriptures and New Testament as Literature have made me sensitive to the nuances of translation into English; consequently, the reader will find that I switch among translations in order to utilize the version that most matches my intentions.

In reflecting over the years about the expression "when the parallel converge," I sometimes could not remember whether the first word was to be "when" or "where." Whether I intended the concept to denote, finally, timelessness or space-lessness sometimes confounded me. Not much remains in my brain from my high-school physics classes, but it does seem to me that, as with parallel lines, there is not only a tangency but also a congruency of time and space in some dimension of understanding. Accordingly, it does not matter which is the first word. What does matter is the understanding, the appreciation, the falling away of the nonessential, the trivial, and the material, the ephemeral in favor of the ineluctable, irreducible, enduring, and inspirited. How to get there? Of what is a pilgrimage made? Lessons, losses, illnesses, love, laughter, the wisdom of and gifts from others, falling down and getting back up, learning to live in God's multicolored, multidimensional, multifaceted creation and seeing that it is both a shadow that is real and a veil that can be pierced to bring the Kingdom of Heaven here and now if only we pause, we smile, we act kindly, and we do rightly. It is for us to discover what abides, what vanishes.

1

Many Waters Cannot Quench Love

Many waters cannot quench love, neither can floods drown it.

Song of Solomon 8:7

i. Flood City

My grandmother loved to drive, but she had certain conditions. She did not drive at night, and she did not drive in bad weather, which in western Pennsylvania meant November to March. The car that I remember my grandmother driving when I first came to live with her was a capacious, charcoal-gray Packard sedan, as old as I was. I could stand on the hump on the floor of the backseat and imperially survey, across the great gray breadth of the hood, the approaching highway and rural scenery. Obviously, no one was thinking about child-restraint seats and seat belts in the 50s and 60s, but my grandmother was, as grandmothers should be, the paragon of safe driving. Her hazel-green eyes were ever scanning the road ahead. We never stopped suddenly. We did not veer unexpectedly. We did not travel at advanced rates of speed and pass everything or anything we might have encountered in a flash of wind and color.

I say "rural" with respect to the scenery, above, because that is the landscape I most remember, though we lived in suburban Johnstown, Pennsylvania. Sunday afternoons after church, after a big dinner at the family-oriented Dairy Dell, we would, as she put it, "explore." We drove through subdivisions sometimes just recently arisen out of pastures and hillsides, but mostly we drove through country lanes, sometimes hunting sights she dimly recalled having seen years before on similar Sunday-afternoon expeditions with other relatives. The nadir of these adventures came for me one afternoon when we followed an increasingly narrow, increasingly rutted lane, while I loudly pleaded throughout that we really were not where we were allowed to be. Suddenly we dead-ended at the flank of a colossal ebony steer. I was, by this time, cowering on the floor of the back seat, with my face cradled in my arms, crying about trespassing (for the very forgiveness of which I had just very attentively prayed in church that very morning) and wild cows. When we backed out of that lane and were securely on a more public two-way route again, my grandmother calmly informed me that it was a bull and was I going to get over it or did we have to go home then and there.

I certainly did not want to go home to our cream-colored ranch house on Sunshine Avenue when there were adventures to be had. We would drive around the reservoir from which our drinking water came, admiring the view and on the lookout for illicit bathers whom we never found; we would drive past Fun City, an amusement park with its enormous, sapphire pool visible from the road, probably two hundred feet above it, its bathers tiny specks of color and activity. We did not stop except when I had a camera, when we would pause long enough that I might snap some pictures that, once developed, were nothing but trees. From the car, however, we could catch sight of the shimmering waters and visualize the peace and tranquility from both vantage points, glimpsing the water through trees. These landscapes we visited also gave me a taste of a larger world beyond my neighborhood horizons, of exciting places to which to travel and about which to learn, imagine, and possess. I yearned to join the swimmers, to participate in their enjoyment of life, and to visit greater lakes and even seas of water and tide.

Once we heard that the Fun City pool had been contaminated and moreover that there really were illegal swimmers in the reservoir, we circuited both, hopeful to espy evidence of illness or examples of the sin of trespass, but to no avail. Nonetheless, it was evident from the frequency with which we returned to these locales that waters were mystical, restorative, even transformative, perhaps, for both of us. It was all part of my education, my growth and development under the guidance of my grandmother, who considered my finishing to be an adult as an important mission. We were checking out the landscape of the world, the places of the physical world that held out the myriad possibilities of life but also, at times, devastation and death.

Years later, when my grandmother had had to turn in her aged Packard for a smaller, more maneuverable, fire-engine red Chevy Nova, we drove the byways looking for rocks for my earth-science project. I did not score very well; I had thirty rocks, misidentifying eight of them, not an estimably accurate percentage. And unlike my classmates' parents who remembered high-school earth science, my grandmother was no help. Surely all any of her children or grandchildren knew about her exposure to science was that she and it did not mix—as a blend or a suspension—and, that, as a freshman at Vassar she had had to take chemistry in a class with all seniors, and consequently it was all right for us to contemplate receiving a "D" in a college subject as she had pioneered for us. However, that grade or lower would not be acceptable at any earlier stage of schooling or presumably in any subject other than science. Well, likely math, too.

Another lesson that my cousins and I learned about Vassar had nothing to do with its educational programs. What we learned how to do was to sing rousingly the anthem of her graduation year, "Twenty-two, twenty-two, twenty-two, we cheer for you!" with the wry second verse, "If it weren't for beer/We wouldn't be here!"

since Matthew Vassar, my grandmother cheerily informed me, was a brewer. (Prohibition, by the way, in the United States, took effect during her college years.) I have my grandmother's college ring now, a gold circlet with the amethyst college seal, reversed and slightly raised in order to serve as sealing-wax stamp, and inscribed with that mystical number. I suspect that my eight cousins, and maybe even some of their spouses or closest friends, can never see the numeral twenty-two and not croon, at least mutely, the hymn of that class, appreciate that collective identity of a group of young women from so long ago. Now we are closer to the hundredth anniversary than to the original date of that graduation, but its spirit endures, the spirit of the exceedingly rare pride of young women who made it through college early in the twentieth century. Moreover, I have since learned that twenty-two is one of the magical numbers of religion—twenty-two generations between Abraham and David, twenty-two generations between David and Jesus. "Twenty-two, twenty-two, twenty-two, we cheer for you!" betokening promise and new life. How apt for a year in which to graduate, to commence. My grandmother ever kept that spirit.

Additionally, my grandmother's English major certainly mattered to her throughout her life, though she reported that the college physician recommended that my grandmother consider medical school after graduation. Surely that doctor did not know of the miserable performance in chemistry. My grandmother would idly speculate about that career choice, at times, though she never said to me that she, on her own initiative, had wanted to be a medical practitioner. She would be a teacher, following the example of her mother Lydia, who had been a teacher in the late 1800s. Lydia, six feet tall, later looming over her grown daughter, a mere five foot five and a half ("Never forget that half!" my grandmother would insist), had nonetheless been intimidated by her overgrown charges as a teacher in a one-room school in backwoods Pennsylvania. Perhaps, in my grandmother, that rare female physician so long ago detected some degree of humaneness, a degree of warmth and compassion that stood at the bedrock of her soul, upon which she drew to be a woman, a parent, a grandparent, a teacher.

Certainly, what my grandmother knew and loved was the study of English, becoming, after her husband died, a high-school literature and grammar teacher and chair of the department at the high school from which I would years later graduate. She was not primarily a student of literature, I suspect, for her notion of English seems to have been primarily grammatical, so much so in fact that when I was very small, dear friends of hers, retired high-school teachers of German and physical education and typing, tried to bribe me to say "ain't" in front of her. But I had had already been scolded, scalded into knowing how terrible it was to say that "A" word. Thus my grandmother's friends were soundly rebuked by my insistence that that was a bad word, never to be uttered, in all probability upon pain of damnation.

The other prohibited word—or phrase—that my grandmother condemned in the English language was "shut up." To say that seemed to her to convey absolute erasure, absolute dissolution and eradication, not just of whatever provocative utterance had occasioned it, evoking such anathema, but to pronounce "shut up" upon someone seemed also to say to the offender not just to be silent but to be scarce, to be gone, and good riddance. I lived in fear that some time I might inadvertently slip and say "shut up!" I suspect I never did, but even now if I ever say it out of exasperation, I am always amazed that the person before me has not disappeared, dissolved like the Wicked Witch of the *Wizard of Oz* but rather is still there and usually still speaking. So much for the power of language these days.

One time, I did involuntarily nearly stumble into that vast otherworld of forbidden speech.

It was late evening; my grandmother and I were both reading in our separate but adjacent bedrooms. I had before me *Black Beauty*, a lovely volume composed out of a repository of truly distinguished English vocabulary. Occasionally, I would consult a dictionary when I came to an unknown term, but the swifter source of information was merely to call out to my grandmother to inquire what a word meant. Accordingly, when I read of a gentleman's waistcoat, from which depended his watch, I hollered, "What's an F. O. B.?"

Pause. No answer.

So I repeated my question.

Finally came my grandmother's voice: "That's a bad word."

I was stunned. What on earth could a bad word have to do with a man's watch? I reread the passage. "Please," I came again. "This is *Black Beauty*. My question has to do with a watch."

Then, she explained that a fob was the watch or the chain or the combination. Whew.

But my grandmother's own linguistic jeopardy over the dangerous waters of forbidden language was not entirely over. Having safely negotiated the fob shoals, I decided to press the point. "What word did you think I said?'

No dice. She did not tell me to shut up, but speaking perhaps one degree less chilling, she commanded, "Never mind." That was generally her final word on a subject to be terminated. It was not as calamitous an execution as "shut up," but it did the job. One cannot be too careful about the treacheries of the English language, I learned.

Notwithstanding that or perhaps because of it, my grandmother's grammatical eye was very helpful with my junior- and senior-high-school themes, the official graders of which seemed principally concerned with spelling and punctuation, too, rather than content or organization or structure or meaning. Thus, I always did very well in English classes after my grandmother had reviewed my work, though she and I would fight like the dickens over the mistakes she located, for I did not take correction lightly. Who was she to say that I had run my sentences too long? Nonetheless, I eventually would adjust my essays as she recommended, but I wanted her to know that it was under extreme protest. She was the first of many editors to try to corral my rambling syntax. She valued writing that was crisp and focused, quite unlike my prolix and meandering style.

My grandmother surely had a keen appreciation for the mother tongue. In fact, she insisted that she was not "raising" me, for I was not, as she said, "a crop of corn or wheat." I was being "reared," and that lesson impressed upon me the distinction of synonyms, that not all words similarly situated in Roget's are equally applicable in all circumstances. What is good for the corn is not good for the child. However, the notion of being reared always conjured for me the image of a graceful, dark stallion up on its hind legs in anger, in revolt. Moreover, now that I think about it, perhaps that was my grandmother's image too—that it is necessary to rear youngsters to be able to rise up against what is wrong, in language, in life, in the world. Reared up meant that we could stand alone against the fates, against the winds, against custom, for ourselves, for what is right, for all time.

O holy cow! Her interests in diction were unrelenting. I can well imagine what my grandmother would make of the squalid language of contemporary popular discourse and culture. That surely would have sent her into high dudgeon. For her, profanity and vulgarity were the unmistakable markers, she judged, of an impoverished vocabulary, for only those who could not come up with interjections and exclamations of vigor and variety would sink to the currency of the realm today, swearing and the language of scatology and sex. Alas.

My grandmother probably came by her interest in language from her own mother, nee Lydia Keller, physically imposing and also witty. My grandmother told me that her mother declared that as the young Miss Keller she had dated both a coffin and a crepe but married a stiff. I did not want, at first, to admit that I did not understand the joke, but eventually I had to ask. I knew what a coffin was, and I knew that my grandmother's maiden name was Stiff, but I thought that otherwise the word was an adjective. Also, I did not know what a crepe was. Thus, my grandmother had to tell me that crepe was funeral ornamentation and that the stiff was, well, the corpse. Thus was there a steady descent, according to Lydia Stiff, in her matrimonial prospects. But no one in our family could ever be accused of impersonating a corpse. We were bred to be lively.

Moreover, as age overtook her, my grandmother would say as her arthritis worsened, albeit with characteristic aplomb, humility, and moderation, "Every morning I awake a little stiff. When I was a child, every morning I was always a little Stiff." So true. Along these lines, my grandmother repeated a maxim of her mother's. It was that God gives each of us exactly slightly more misfortune or burdens or trouble than we can bear. How right that often seems. Similarly, my grandmother offered her own adage: "Moderation in all things, including moderation." We are to judge, therefore, the aptness of our behavior in all circumstances.

Of her husband's family, the Raabs (pronounced *robs*), my grandmother informed me that there was one side that was good-looking and rich, whereas our side, the good side, was witty and intelligent. It took me many years to appreciate the value of that distribution. I was, for many years, stalled on the verdict that evidently I lacked beauty, while society all around me extolled that trait, but it was clear that the family values that mattered were to be funny and smart, and my grandmother, married into that tribe, set the tone. Vivacity was all.

I remember my grandmother's telling me, too, that her mother had told of the time that her younger sister Martha, last in birth order after brother Will, who followed Lydia, had come into their older sister's room one morning before Lydia had gotten up, snuggled in bed with her, and whispered, "Lydia, did that nice Mr. Stiff come to visit last evening?" On receiving an affirmative answer, which had made Lydia smile to think how promising it was that Martha liked her beau, Martha, in turn, smiled and further inquired, "And did he bring a box of chocolates again?"

"Yes, he did."

To which answer, Martha rose up from the bed and shouted, "Yes, Will!"

Not surprisingly, then, in light of the merit placed by both sides of the family upon intelligence and wit, my grandmother was a great reader. She consumed the local daily newspaper and select magazines—the Johnstown *Tribune-Democrat*, *Reader's Digest*, *US News and World Report*, journals from the American Association of Retired Persons and the National Retired Teachers Association and the American Association of University Women (AAUW)—but she did not read poetry or, very frequently, novels. And I was perturbed because we did not subscribe to anything well illustrated—like *Life* or *Look* or *The Saturday Evening Post*—which I could pillage to illustrate usefully, whether appropriately or not, history or geography projects. I remember that my grandmother did not read *In Cold Blood* when it came out because she had heard the rabbi of the local Beth Zion Temple term it trash. She read *The Greening of America*, a progressive critique that I imagine must have caused a philosophic dissonance with the traditional values of the *Digest*, but she did not discuss it with me at any length.

Mostly in the evenings we watched a little television—she loved Westerns, while I held out for espionage adventures, and she wrote letters to her college roommates in California, Wisconsin, and Virginia; to her distant cousins; and to her two surviving children and their families, established in Ohio and Pittsburgh and then Virginia. That last included particularized replies to grandchildren, who had most likely been coerced into writing to her in the first place, correspondence from them that she would return with all the spelling and punctuation infelicities corrected in red ink. It did not endear her to them. And she wrote regularly to my father in far-off New Jersey, to confirm for him the wise and prudent superintending of my upbringing and the judicious expending of the seventy-five dollars she received every month from him for that purpose.

On weekends we played cards. We played a game called Spite and Malice—what a lesson for a child—and when I went to high school and joined the Bridge Club, we played a version of honeymooners' or two-handed bridge for hours at a time on weekend afternoons. She regularly played genuine, contract bridge with two groups of retired teachers, including those women who had tried to lead my vocabulary astray. My grandmother claimed that she was neither mathematical nor competitive, but against my beginners' luck, her bridge game was calculating, precise, and ruthless.

Together we also played Parcheesi, which she loved, and which she claimed she had played with five generations of family, having been taught it by her grandfather, former Union Captain William Keller, father of Lydia Stiff, who had learned it during his unfortunate tenure as a prisoner of war in Libby Prison outside Richmond—although we later learned, when my uncle Harry did research at the National Archives, that the revered Captain was more often a private and a corporal and an occasional sergeant and that his military career was distinguished by as many downward trajectories as promotions. Nonetheless, he had clearly prospered as a champion Parcheesi player, a game I found rather dreary compared to more interesting contests such as Monopoly, Clue, Life, or Careers or even, for a brief spell, the Barbie game, though my grandmother could not abide such silly, dressed-up, convoluted competitions.

Probably the principal favored board game at my house, which my cousins also enjoyed when they came to visit, was the Ouija board. My grandmother averred that she firmly believed in extrasensory perception. I remember one time hearing my cousin David say to his sister, "I know you were pushing it, Sibyl! If I don't die when I'm ninety-two, I'll know it is your fault!" Well, he is still alive, though not yet ninety two. However, my grandmother and I also spent endless hours pushing or not pushing the prototype mouse around the board, painstakingly spelling out fortunes and fates. My grandmother allowed the interrogation of the board to focus on what I wanted to know: "Will I get at least a 'B' in Math?" "Where will I go to college?" "Will I write a book?" But now I wonder if she were not hoping also to hear from some of the many beloved whom she had buried, if she were not trying to pierce the veil to the otherworld, to spirits who might be trying to get in touch with us? Her parents, her husband, and my mother all died within a single decade, leaving her, an only child, for a time likely nearly emotionally abandoned.

We frequented two restaurants on Sundays after church. As the widow of a former executive at Johnstown's Bethlehem Steel plant, she could dine at the exclusive Ye Olde Country Club, but more often we went to the Dairy Dell, which did not serve alcohol. My grandmother was not much of an imbiber, so that probably did not trouble her. She drank sherry when the occasion warranted an alcoholic beverage, but in general, it seemed, much time would pass without liquor touching her lips, except, of course, at the monthly Eucharist at our Episcopal church. Thus, it was with some trepidation but much anticipation that when I came home from college at Christmas during my senior year, having at last turned of legal drinking age according to Pennsylvania dictum, I hatched my plot. One morning when we made an expedition to the supermarket, I encouraged her to buy a carton of the premixed eggnog beverage. When we got home, I suggested that I visit the Pennsylvania State Store nearby, since I was now twenty-one, to buy some rum to accompany it. She agreed, and when I got home, I placed the eggnog and the rum on the kitchen counter.

"What proportions do you suppose we should use to make the drink?" I asked. I had a pretty good idea, but I was curious to see what she might say.

"Oh, equal," she replied confidently.

Well, she was not someone with whom to disagree, so I dutifully filled our tall, *Wizard of Oz* iced-tea glasses half full of rum and half full of eggnog.

As we drank and compared notes on our respective collegiate days, I watched her face growing rosier and rosier. I decided unhappily but drunkenly that I had probably killed her. "Would you like another?" I inquired.

"Oh, sure," she said. "That just hit the spot."

My grandmother loved holidays, though certain ones were more important than others. Her younger daughter pointed out to me once that her mother's March birthday and some remote Anglo Irish ancestry therefore made her especially fond of St. Patrick's Day, for which my grandmother would pin a pipe-cleaner shamrock to her clothes. She also seemed greatly moved by patriotic days. We had a flag holder on the wall next to the garage door and always suspended the American banner there for that rash of warm-weather commemorations—Memorial Day, Flag Day, and the Fourth of July. It was grand to drive off and see the flag gaily waving, though frequently we came home to find it drooping onto the driveway. My grandmother and I would then confer over whether or not we should observe what she said was proper flag protocol and burn the flag since it had touched the ground. Her sense of patriotic propriety here clearly warred with her notion of what she, the inveterate coupon clipper, called her Scotchness, sometimes termed frugality or stinginess. Universally, we decided if the flag looked clean it was probably all right, this time.

I think that my grandmother loved Christmas most of all, though she said it was a melancholy time of year because so many of her loved ones had died in the fall: her parents, my mother, but especially closest to the holiday season her husband, who passed away the very week of Christmas years before, before any of my cousins, their grandchildren, were born. Christmas was perhaps special because it can be so bittersweet, combining grief and pleasure together, inextricably. I remember one time at her son's house; she and I and my three cousins who lived there were sitting on their L-shaped couch in the family room. My grandmother announced, "I know where the presents are!" It did not take much teasing to elicit that she had discovered a cache of gifts poorly hidden, as it turned out, beneath the sofa upon which she was so regally ensconced. Her triumphant discovery, it seemed to me at the time, had the high spirits of a child.

One of the landmarks of life in the vicinity of Johnstown when I was growing up was shopping at the signal department store, Penn Traffic, especially around Christmas. Evidently, this peculiarly named emporium still exists as a supermarket chain in the Northeast, but in the day, the term denominated the high-rise splendor —that is, mounting all of five stories—of the dominant department store in Johnstown. It had been, my grandmother told me, originally the company store of Bethlehem Steel, the corporation that made Johnstown, and now it reposed at the end of Johnstown, aside one of the rivers, between a fire station and office buildings of the headquarters of the Johnstown Plant, Bethlehem Steel.

When I was very young, Penn Traffic was where I was deposited for several successive years on Santa's lap to have my picture taken and to pass on my list of worldly desiderata. And it was at this festive time that this department store, maybe all stores, truly comes into its own. At Christmastide in my childhood, the large plate-glass windows of Penn Traffic were of course filled with exhibits of fashionably clad mannequins to entice shoppers inside, but the display inside one window, at the very end of the block-long store, for many Christmas seasons featured an imitation-snow-covered, animated display. There might be Santa and the elves, maybe, a train, maybe a Dickensian village, something with moving parts, just as the big department stores in New York and Pittsburgh had as I saw years later, drawing crowds who jiggled and pressed close to examine, to exclaim over, to enjoy. It was an imaginary landscape of Yuletide dreams come to life, created to beguile shoppers to come in out of the cold. And we willingly did, once we had seen our fill, observed all the movements. We would turn to the doors, ascend a flight of steps into the warm, inviting air of the store and its counters and racks of beautiful, desirable merchandise. This was most unlike what my grandmother disdained as Penn Traffic's working-class competitor, in which customers bustled into a first floor odiferous with the scent of freshly roasted peanuts and newly popped corn, cheap, tawdry, my grandmother would surely sniff. Rather, Penn Traffic exuded heavenly calm and cleanliness, encouraging thoughtful, careful investment in purchases designed to last, not in easy-to-come, easy-to-go snacks.

At Christmases, on a two-story-tall wall at one end of the first floor of Penn Traffic for many years hung huge tapestries of holiday scenes, vast carpets of crimson, mulberry, cinnamon, pumpkin, and chocolate tones, illustrating seasonal themes, like Santa's workshop or the Nativity, other imaginary landscapes, which complemented the feeling of warmth and comfort of the department store against the cold winds outside, though the carpets disappeared one autumn a long time ago and never returned. Beneath them, as long as they lasted, probably in November, my grandmother and I would select our Christmas cards, paging through vast, bulging scrapbooks of multitudes of cards of every design and picture imaginable, from which we would select our own and order them with our names engraved inside. Why I needed to have my name mechanically inscribed on the contents of the single box of twenty-five I was getting, I cannot conceive, but my grandmother would have her name added to the four or five boxes she selected for herself, and she saw nothing wrong with my following her example. I was being schooled, of course, in the art of sending Christmas cards, of maintaining connections, of living in a world of human contact. And we would also buy several Chanukah cards to send as well. The mothers of my Jewish friends who received them often called my grandmother to thank her for Laura's thoughtfulness. But I knew who truly deserved the gratitude.

Penn Traffic, as you see, looms very large in my childhood memories of my grandmother. It was a kind of nirvana, a touchstone offering wares that promised travel and excitement to distant lands from whence its merchandise came. This was a counterpoint of exploration to our Sunday travels made at warmer times of the year.

As I grew up, we would frequently go to Penn Traffic on Saturdays, lunching in its dining room before spending the afternoon shopping. Saturdays gave us the world of the material, while then on Sundays our weekends would be completed by church and the world of the spirit.

Usually, we would arrive at the store to begin our expedition with lunch, but one time we were later than usual, and my grandmother greatly embarrassed me. Hungrily, we waited in line beside a low wall topped by a short glass window, on the other side of which were diners, including two obviously off-duty waitresses, evidenced by their uniforms, who were chatting and smoking, but conspicuously not eating. They were probably enjoying their break, but that was insufficient for my grandmother's sense of indignation and outrage at their lack of compassion and hospitality. She huffed in a stage whisper, but to my ears so loudly that everyone in Johnstown might hear, "I can't imagine sitting there smoking while people are standing in line starving for lunch." To my grandmother, I imagine, had Moses lived several thousand years later, he would have had the wit to add an eleventh commandment, "Thou shalt not smoke." Thus, these waitresses epitomized sloth, selfishness, and lack of fellow feeling, all summed up for my grandmother in the billows of smoke escaping from their mouths. Given that disposition, I was very surprised, years later, to learn that her husband, my grandfather, had smoked. I do not know how she stood it.

Alas, the Penn Traffic department store expired following the 1976 Johnstown flood. The domestic steel industry after its World War II and postwar successes was collapsing, taking Johnstown's fortunes in general down with it. In the 1976 flood, built there right next to the river, the lower floors of Penn Traffic were swamped with water, and the grand store never reopened. Indeed, Johnstown was a failing city throughout my childhood, and the mountains that surrounded it, hemming us in, gave me a sense in general of decline, destitution, and depression, claustrophobic, I thought then, oppressive, though the splendors of Penn Traffic yet linger in my favorite Christmas memories. It abides as the epitome of the material world, offering rich wares from faraway if not glamorous places, tempting us to buy, to indulge the physical self in the worldly yet also the transient.

In my grandmother's world, transgressions were linked. If a person erred in one area, there were undoubtedly other sins for which to account, as well. The transgression of smoking, therefore, might well be connected to linguistic vice. This became apparent one time, when in idle conversation I said something innocently introduced by the expression, "Like I said. . ."

Whoosh! The waters of the Great Johnstown Flood or the trump of final judgment could not have descended with more mercilessness upon me than did the wrath of my grandmother for that grammatical infraction. "Where did you pick that up?" she demanded since she knew I had never learned it in her presence.

Not being one to take the blame for another and rouse my grandmother's ire, I swiftly offered up an elementary-school teacher for grammatical execution. And she never again respected that teacher. Moreover, that grammatical infraction opened up for my grandmother a new front in her unremitting warfare against smoking (which even resulted ultimately in her selling her profitable Nabisco stock when the company was bought by R. J. Reynolds). This time, though, her rage against tobacco merged with her campaign for the proper use of English, and she constantly inveighed against the slogan, "Winston tastes good like a cigarette should." She harrumphed at the weak company excuse when others of like mind objected and were told it was "folksy."

"What kind of useful condition is 'folksiness'?" my grandmother queried. I never knew if her questions were rhetorical or demanded a response, but I certainly knew better than to try to disagree with her on these points.

"Why would anyone smoke," she demanded, "Knowing that the mother tongue was being humiliated by the company?" Who dared to disagree?

Consequently, I found smoking the chief vehicle of my adolescent rebellion. When I went off to college and lived among other young people for the first time in my life, I gloried in the license of youth, at the time celebrated by the 1970's media already nostalgic for 1960's hedonism and self-indulgence. So I smoked. And, for the most part, most of my friends did too, which was part of my self-justification.

But naturally I hid my filthy noxious habit, or tried to, when I went home, until the summer after I had graduated from college, and I was home for three months before leaving for graduate school. One day, some weeks into my sojourn, my grandmother said, "I don't know why your clothes still have the smell of tobacco in them. They've been washed several times now. Your roommate must have been a chimney."

I could no longer let Amy, even unbeknownst to her, bear the burden of such guilt, though probably she would have been unfazed or even amused by it, and I confessed. "It is not Amy's smoking you smell. It's mine."

My grandmother said nothing. She turned on her heel and stormed to her room, slamming the door. She stayed there for several hours and, when she emerged, was very frosty for some time. I was mortified, but I was also willful and stubborn. I continued to smoke, but never in my grandmother's presence, only in my car and late at night out the bathroom window, until I went off to Bryn Mawr in the fall. From then, I smoked and smoked and smoked for a decade, though my grandmother railed against the practice in her weekly letters and phone calls. Not one of my finer moments. She did finally concede that my mother had smoked, too, but, said my grandmother, "She was smart enough to quit." Eventually, so was I.

When my grandmother and I were at home for Christmas, she always served turkey. The reason was that sometime in early November she would always say to me, if we were not going to visit her son or daughter for Thanksgiving, "Oh, do you really want a turkey this year? They are such a nuisance to fuss with. What if we just go out to dinner for Thanksgiving?" So we would dine out, either at Dairy Dell, or once to another restaurant more beatifically named Shangri-La, where we marveled at the empty dining room and the full parking lot. Shortly after we left, the police raided the restaurant's basement for gambling. However, after Thanksgiving, she would start to pine for leftover turkey, so she would fret with the holiday fowl for Christmas.

My grandmother did not enjoy cooking, and accordingly I never learned my way around a kitchen from her. She said, "I cooked for twenty years while I was married, and now I don't have to do it anymore." For that reason, we ate a lot of frozen dinners and her one specialty, Spanish rice, made of catsup and instant rice. She prided herself as well on her British gustatory preferences: meat and potatoes. However, I was long under the impression that mashed potatoes were derived from flakes in a box, unembellished with gravy, butter, or anything else. We did not own a spice rack, and she rarely if ever used salt and pepper. She would fix roasts, though, especially on the Sundays when my father came to visit.

They were well-done without sauce or accompaniment other than frozen vegetables.

While my mouth watered at the homemade cookies and cakes at my cousins' homes, we never baked, and my grandmother stored boxes of breakfast cereal and crackers in the little-used oven to keep them away from ants. However, that did lead to a calamity one Christmas when I decided to try to make gingerbread men. I turned on the oven to preheat it without looking inside first, and, as the kitchen filled with a bitter, acrid smoke, I discovered that my oversight had ignited a small conflagration of cardboard and crackers. The experience was not redeemed when I subsequently burned the cookies, as well.

Not only was my grandmother patriotic, as her devotion to the American flag shows, she was also religious. For my tenth birthday, she gave me a King James' Version of the Bible with Jesus's words in red letters and the binding of the book closed with a zipper attached to a small cross. I still keep it beside my bed. We went to church every Sunday except in bad weather. We sat in the second row on the left side of the central aisle so that I could easily recess with the other children for Sunday school when we would be led out before the sermon.

Ours was a small, lovely Gothic church. It had been built about a decade before the turn of the twentieth century, to replace one lost in the Great Johnstown Flood of 1889, in which had drowned the rector Lorenzo Potter Diller and his wife and children, as well as my grandmother's grandmother-in-law and two of her husband's aunts, one of whose bodies was never recovered, but that's another story. The altar and some of the stained-glass windows of St. Mark's Church had been donated in the memory of the Dillers. When I came forward for communion once a month, I would read, carved in the paneling at the altar, "Many waters cannot quench love."

As I approached junior-high-school age, I asked my grandmother when I could be confirmed. I said I was eager to drink the wine. She said that such an attitude was sacrilegious, and clearly I was not yet ready. However, she relented when it appeared that all the little girls and boys my age were to be confirmed that year. All the other girls had brand-new pure white dresses. I, on the other hand, already possessed what my grandmother termed a perfectly good, generally white dress, but it was flawed, to my way of thinking, by a big purple iris that sprang up one side out of some hemline vegetation. However, I believed that if I hunched over and extended my left arm straight down so that my hand gripped the hem, no one would see the flower, so that was how I marched into church. I was more concerned, in any case, that God was going to refuse to accept me in my slough of immense sinfulness with a grand peal of thunder at the moment that Bishop Austin Pardue of the Diocese of Pittsburgh laid his ancient seraphic hands upon my head. And I was astonished when the Bishop approached me, lowered his hands, placed them on my head, spoke his blessing, and confirmed me as one of Christ's own, that there was silence. No thunder. No peal of rejection. I was astounded and gratified at my reprieve by grace.

As I was growing up, my grandmother persuaded me that we were poor Appalachians. Johnstown's failing fortunes certainly contributed to that sense. And I had no reason to doubt her labeling since I had nothing with which or with whom to compare. We were clearly poorer than people on TV, it seemed to me, and because we always had only one aging car and were always having to turn out lights when we were not in rooms, could not protract long-distance phone calls, and did not splurge on toys, candy, movies, going out to eat except on weekends, and on vacations to Europe or Hawaii, I was willing enough to believe we were impoverished. Plus, we did not belong to the Sunnehanna Country Club, at least partly because my grandmother did not play golf. I did not question the fact that she did not need to go to work to have an income; she received mysterious checks from insurance, investments, Social Security, and my father, which apparently paid our bills, although just barely, I assumed. Furthermore, surely enough, we lived in the Allegheny Mountains of southwestern Pennsylvania. The woman across the street pointed out that the last four digits of our phone number, 2743, constituted the elevation of the

Laurel Mountain that we crossed on our way to Pittsburgh between Johnstown and Old Fort Ligonier of the French and Indian War, so we were certainly at an exalted elevation of mountainousness. Additionally, once we had cable—much later, though—and could get the sophisticated and alien Pittsburgh television stations, like all our neighbors who had had seemingly expensive antennas for years—it was evident that our outside temperatures were always cooler because we "were in the mountains." Consequently, I believed I was a poor Appalachian, rather than just the grandchild of a frugal woman. Of course, I had no notion of hollows and cabins and outdoor latrines and gas lighting and all the other virtues of mountain living. The closest I came to all that was summer camp, which I despised.

Johnstown is a bowl in the mountains, which is the feature that enabled the Great Johnstown Flood to nearly destroy it. Both my grandmother and I grew up in the shadows of the Great Flood. There were at least three floods historically that merited the title, and apparently in the 1800s there had been recurrent, frequent, but unremarkable ones, before Johnstown was married to the word "flood" forever more. In 1936, there was a flood that was supposed to have been the last flood ever, around St. Patrick's Day, in which melting snow caused the banks of the Little Stonycreek and Conemaugh Rivers to overflow. Johnstown had been founded at their confluence, just like a miniature Pittsburgh, toward which the soon-to-be conjoined waters of Johnstown in due course flowed. According to my grandmother, Franklin Delano Roosevelt came to Johnstown in 1936 with his wheelchair and his cigarette lighter and threw federal money at the riverbanks, which were cemented and concreted over to prevent ever after another flood. And the flood prevention lasted, until the national Bicentennial month and year of July, 1976, when a foot of rain fell out of the sky. Seventy to eighty people drowned then. Many more than died in 1936, and worse property damage occurred. My grandmother remembered the rains of both of these floods, though she lived on the hilltops overlooking the city and was out of harm's way each time.

City Hall in downtown Johnstown had for some time—though I have not been back in years to confirm this fact—three water marks on it, way over the heads of people walking past, to indicate how deep the waters were in the three floods. Clearly the worst of all was the day after traditional Memorial Day, 1889, when it seemed that all the material world had washed away in a cataclysm as in the pages of the Bible.

I want to tell a story about a valley between two mountains where the waters flowed too high, too deep, and too fast, where the rains came and the dam broke, and the flood waters rushed away trees and trains and houses and people, where the old stone bridge at the two rivers' convergence became another dam, a cruel and frightening barrier of sticks and stones and debris and detritus, maybe, in fact, just like South Fork Dam all over again, but here it was a dam of fire and not of water. The fuel from the wrecked trains piled up there as the bridge caught fire, and everything burned, so where there had been flood there now was fire.

How does the world end? Does it end in fire and flood? I want to know, did God call their names when the people cried and screamed? Did he wrap his arms around the mothers and children and brothers and sisters and fathers and lonely folks as they writhed and suffered and gave up their ghosts? Are they in his arms now: Did many fires stanch his care? Did many waters quench his love?

That flood was caused by the collapse, under the pressure of two days of heavy, steady, pounding rainfall, of the South Fork Dam at the South Fork Hunting and Fishing Club a bit northwest and disastrously upstream from Johnstown. The Club consisted of Henries Clay and Frick, Andrews Carnegie and Mellon, and other rich Pittsburghers, who never paid a penny to Johnstown in reparation or remorse for the damage caused by their ill-maintained earthen dam, which created their boating lake. Visit the wonderful art collection Mellon gave to the nation and to the Smithsonian to sense the size of the unshared riches from which devastated, wiped-out Johnstown was deprived. It is yet possible to drive around the area of that private club to see the still standing so-called cottages, huge Victorian mansions, in which these well-to-do people from Pittsburgh summered.

In any case, just before the summer of 1889, the dam gave way, and its lake waters surged downstream to Johnstown, killing over two thousand people—drowned or burned when the old stone bridge at the two rivers' convergence erupted in flames. The water came charging down the riverbed, toward Pittsburgh, picking up trees, debris, people, buildings, train cars, absolutely everything in its path, and when it encountered the bridge, it washed backward, flooding Johnstown a second time, and then again, this time abandoning all its collateral matter at the bridge, where that piled-up concatenation burst into flames and burned in a mighty conflagration of wooden, combustible debris, trapping victims who had not, mercifully, drowned in the calamity, but were now to perish by fire.

Many images of the flood exist. The pictures of postdiluvian Johnstown are of planks and mud and boards and mountains of debris. No buildings are seen standing. A famous picture shows a pitched-over house with a huge elm or walnut tree sticking out of it, its roots in the air and the house on its side. A train crossing Pennsylvania from Philadelphia to Pittsburgh, filled with people who had no connection whatsoever with Johnstown, stranded its passengers there when the tracks washed out, and then all were drowned or burned in the Great Johnstown Flood. Washed away. Bodies were found as far away as the Ohio River six months later.

Memorable events happened in the Flood. A little boy survived because his head was caught in the banister of the stairs of his house, forever deforming his face as the price of his salvation. A baby was born during that terrible night, who was named Harry Flood Something-or-Other. Clara Barton came to town and brought the Red Cross, which pitched tents and passed out blankets along with bulky clothes. As I have said, a great-great grandmother of mine, on the other side of the family from my grandmother's, drowned along with two sisters and her mother. Her daughter, my great grandmother, newly married and moved to the safe sanctuary of her new husband's home on higher ground, survived. My grandmother said that this woman, her mother-in-law, never talked about the flood, never recalled for others that trying, horrific night and its devastating aftermath.

My grandmother's mother Lydia, her mother, father Captain Keller from the Civil War, and her younger brother and sister Will and Martha lived through that stormy, turbulent night. As the waters climbed their staircase, they retreated to the attic, where they huddled in the cold and the dark while outside the gale raged. The next morning when they crept downstairs and peeked outside, they saw ruination and calamity, catastrophe and apocalypse. Virtually nothing was left standing. All was rubble, ruin, wreckage where on sunny days a prosperous nineteenth-century downtown of storefronts and houses, wagons, horses, tradesmen, laborers, women, and children, colorful, shouting to and greeting one another, had flourished. Surely, the Kellers and the other survivors must have thought, it was the end of the world, but an indomitable spirit also made it the birth of another, since the survivors rebuilt their lives, their homes, and their town, on the flood plain. That is their story. That is their truth.

My grandmother and I attended annual banquets in commemoration of the flood, which were held on the floor of the cavernous community center called the War Memorial. Harry Flood Something-or-Other would get up to expound that he had no recollections of the flood, at which everyone would laugh. Frozen, implacable, black-and-white slides of the damage would be shown.

In Grandview Cemetery where my mother and now my grandmother are buried there are seven hundred seventy-seven small tablets of limestone lined up in rows behind a pedestal on which stands an angel. These are the bodies of the never identified victims of the Great Johnstown Flood, including those of one of my great-great aunts. Her mother's and sister's bodies were recovered and buried in the Raab family plot. The flood memorial is a strikingly placid place.

Two museums now memorialize the disaster, each with its own frightening video of the rush of water, the cascade of catastrophe, the Niagara of nightmares. One of these documentaries won an Oscar. My grandmother never wanted to see the films, but on our Sunday-afternoon outings we would sometimes drive by the scene of the dam on an interstate, suspended high over where the South Fork Hunting and Fishing Club lakebed was, and my grandmother would slow almost to a stop so that we could gaze in awe at two motionless, grassy cliffs facing each other over a deep and wide ravine, which was where the traitorous earthen dam stood and then fell in upon itself under the relentless, remorseless pounding of the rain. That Memorial Day, more than a foot of water had fallen to cause the ill-tended dam to give way.

Many waters cannot quench love.

I remember the only time that I saw my grandmother cry.

Appropriately, perhaps, it was the eve of my departure for college. She had not cried in my presence when our four-year-old cat Fluffy died, though I sobbed and begged for another. She responded, "No, it is too sad when they die." She did not cry in my presence when I would come home from playing with neighbor children, bawling, "They made fun of me and called me 'Fatty,'" though she would call their parents and oblige the miscreants to come to the door of our house to apologize.

More to the point perhaps, she did not cry in my presence when, one by one, all her friends began to die, starting with the death of her best friend Phoebe Davies when I was not yet in school but still old enough to form a memory of that occasion I could summon later. As it happens, almost as much as I was ever informed about the facts of life from my grandmother concerned Phoebe Davies.

One day my grandmother said to me, rather out of the blue, when I was probably in high school, "Do you know what a vagina is?"

I gulped and affirmed.

I should have known. The reason she asked was not some deep embarrassment about sexual knowledge that she was about to unleash but rather that she was about to tell me a funny story.

For then she said, "Do you remember my friend Phoebe Davies?"

And upon her receipt of a second affirmative, she continued, "One day when the vacuum-cleaner salesman came to her door—you know that that is how vacuum cleaners used to be sold, like Fuller Brush and Avon products—she meant to tell him that she had already a Regina with which she was satisfied, but instead she dispatched him, in more ways than one, probably, by declaring, 'No thank you. I already have a vagina.'"

We guffawed, and I have since wondered what the salesman thought.

Back to the night before I left for college, when the living room was strewn with boxes and suitcases, my grandmother; my father, who would drive me to college the next day; and I were dining in the ell of the cluttered living room. In plain view of my collegiate-bound chattels, we had stumbled through our customary shambles that passed for conversation, until it became time for dessert. My father declined dessert, deferring to later, as was his wont. Off to the kitchen I went to scoop ice cream for my grandmother and me. I returned with two bowls: the modest scoop or so that I knew was her desired portion and the heaping mounds that would slake my appetite.

My father rose up in fury, probably containing all his fears and anxieties about this next stage in my and their lives: "Omigod! You are not going to eat all that, are you?"

I was aghast. I was humiliated. I was scared, with all my fears and anxieties equally aroused in that moment.

I rose from the table and stormed off, headed for what until that weekend had been the direction of my bedroom. Unfortunately, in my distress, I had forgotten that my grandmother had now moved into my first-floor, larger room; my father was ensconced for his visit in the small, now guest room which had been through my childhood my grandmother's room, and I was now installed, for my absence, for all eternity, in the opposite direction from which I had fled, in the spare room over the garage. All I had before me, however, in the direction in which I was headed was the bathroom. I could not turn around, retrace my steps to get to my new bedroom, and face him again. So I scuttled into the bathroom and shut the door. I could not lock it because my grandmother had removed the internal locks from the doors to the bathroom and my bedroom when I was a child so that I could never lock myself away. I sat on the edge of the tub in despair, fully prepared to remain there until they both died and their skeletons were left at the dining room table.

A tentative knock came at the door. I cannot remember if I opened the door, if it opened of its own accord, or if I said, "Come in." But suddenly there was my grandmother, bearing the bowl of ice cream, tears streaming down her face. "I tried to rear you right," she wailed.

I nodded, but then I shook my head at the proffered bowl of ice cream. "I cannot eat that." The door closed on my grandmother and the bowl. She had never before cried in my presence. I do not recall how long I sat there, but eventually I must have left. However, none of us ever discussed the event. I would like to say we never ate ice cream again, but I cannot.

Several hours later, when I was taking my last bath ever in that bathtub—since I was bound for who knows what might befall me once I left home for college and the rest of my life—I leaned back, as I always did, sinking into the bathtub and placing my feet between the faucet and the hot and cold water handles. This time, unfortunately, that action sent one of my feet through the wall into the linen closet beyond. I heard plaster and wallboard fall through the wall and the obviously infirm floor there into the basement below. It was an evening of horrors! I was leaving home, and the house was collapsing in my wake.

Interestingly, my grandmother was not demonstrably angry when I confessed shortly thereafter, though she, an inveterate tub bather, blamed the wall's weakness on all the showers I had taken over the years.

ii. Mrs. Raab

My grandmother was a dyed-in-the-wool Yankee. Not a New England Yankee, but the Pennsylvania variety. Her mother had belonged to the Daughters of the American Revolution (DAR), but for whatever reason my grandmother did not feel inspired to join herself. She told me at one point not to believe any of the rumors that she had not joined because she was adopted. I cannot imagine where she thought I might hear such rumors. Nonetheless, she resembled too clearly the pictures of her parents to have been adopted, in any case. However, perhaps she held back from the DAR because her singular patriotic loyalty was to the American Civil War of her grandfather, what I, now having lived in the South for more than a quarter century, have come to know from white old-timers here, as the War of Northern Aggression. Despite her partisan loyalty to the North, she was fascinated by the South and surely is not surprised from wherever she is now serenely surveying mortal affairs that I have stayed planted in the red-clay soil of this endlessly captivating and paradoxical part of the nation this past nearly half century and beyond.

Five times when I was a child, her son my Uncle Harry, his wife, and their three children from Pittsburgh took my grandmother and me along on their summer-vacation trips. And what trips they were. Once we went north on an arc that reached from the Thousand Islands of the St. Lawrence River, where my grandmother had gone on her honeymoon, to the Maritime Provinces of Canada, where we saw the tidal bore at St. John's and the Bay of Fundy off New Brunswick, with stops in Ottawa and Montreal and Quebec in between, and then down homeward through Maine and Boston. In 1966 we traveled to the New York World's Fair with stops at Gettysburg and Philadelphia en route. In New York we stayed at the Vassar Club on Lexington Avenue. But our two earliest vacations were to Nags Head, North Carolina, and all the Civil War battlefields and memorials between Pennsylvania and the Tar Heel State—Antietam, Shiloh, Appomattox Court House.

But all these summer expeditions culminated in one mammoth three-week-long drive out West, ultimately to San Francisco, pausing at as many of the national parks along a wide northern trip outward and a descending semicircle for our return as we could, to such places as the Grand Canyon, the Painted Desert, Yosemite,

Zion, Bryce Canyon, Grand Teton, Yellowstone, and Mount Rushmore, along with Salt Lake City and other locales along the way, showcasing the rich diversity of American geography and culture. I was much taken with the Mormon experience, which I suspect is a large part of the purpose of the Salt Lake City tour guide's enthusiasm, and bought a Book of Mormon and might nearly have converted if my grandmother had not asserted her Episcopal will and reminded me of the true Anglican faith of our family. Nonetheless, for the trip as a whole, how my education expanded. Geography, history, places, people all unfolded before my eyes and ears. Four children, two parents, one mother-in-law in a station wagon, the journey might have been a tale along the lines of "A Good Man Is Hard to Find" but without the cat and the Misfit. I later much admired my aunt and uncle for having generously included a fourth child and my strong-willed grandmother.

When Uncle Harry and Aunt Phebe were planning that longest trip and making reservations at all the Holiday Inns where we would stay, they needed to know for certain if my grandmother and I were coming. Consequently, my grandmother needed to secure my father's acquiescence, so her parsimonious soul sent him a parsimonious telegram, for which she carefully counted out the characters: "Have chance to go west. Stop. Please advise. Stop. Mother Raab."

When my father called, on no doubt immediate receipt of the terse telegram, he was a bit speechless. He admitted that he had not inferred from the truly telegraphic message a three-week trip to the West Coast staying at Holiday Inns along the way. I tried to get him to disclose what he had thought my grandmother was cabling, but he would not say. Relentlessly, I bedeviled my grandmother for some time trying to ferret out a possible interpretation from her, but she finally said she did not want to talk about the matter anymore. Never mind.

My cousins and I entertained ourselves on that trip playing one three-week-long game of Hearts, which I believe that ultimately I won, though perhaps each of them now also remembers having triumphed, so that as we drove through the desolate and barren wastelands of Idaho, looking across vast, empty expanses for sites that my uncle said were connected with his work for the Navy and Admiral Rickover, his immediate supervisor, my grandmother said, interrupting our intense card play, "Laura, you need to look out the windows so you can tell your grandchildren what you have seen."

"Don't my cousins have to look out the window, too?"

"I have no control over them."

"Well, I am not planning to have any grandchildren." And I did not and do not. But nonetheless great images from that landscape endure in my mind, of the wider world that my education was expanding to include.

We spent many long days in the car on that trip west. Some days we drove as many as six hundred miles across the pavements of the interstate system, blowing past the differentials of American landscape—dusty, mountainous, forested, empty, wide, clear, open, sometimes with tumbleweed, from Iowa cornfields and western Badlands, to desert and towns, sometimes land so still that I could try to imagine the decades of pioneers that had left their imprint, their traces, their breath in the air and on the ground. These travels were the final incarnations of those journeys on Sunday afternoons with my grandmother when we explored the landscape around Johnstown. Now, our paths crossed the continent and all the mysteries and unknown places that it held and promised.

In Yellowstone, where we were enthralled to see bison and one morning an elk and calf in the backyard of our cabin and one time a bear and three cubs along the roadside, we were excited at another juncture to see snow along the roadside in July. One other car had stopped to spill its passengers to witness at close hand such a miracle. We were all amused to discover that it was also a carload of Pennsylvanians, the last people who should have been amazed at snow, no matter the season. Perhaps the mystery here was in the familiar and not the strange.

Besides Hearts, we kiddos, as my uncle called us, would play other games. In Yellowstone, we were entranced by the boardwalks that covered unstable ground because of the volcano deep within the surface of the earth, boardwalks to circumvent the hot springs and geysers along the way. Roaming across the boardwalks made my cousins and me think of the yellow brick road. Accordingly, we all assumed travel identities from *The Wizard of Oz*: my oldest cousin Connie chose Dorothy for herself; her brother Harry and sister Cynthie were the Tin Man and the Scarecrow; for being a Leo I claimed the nom de guerre of the Cowardly Lion. My uncle Harry was most usefully Uncle Henry, but then we had some difficulties for the two adult women. Mischievously, two of my cousins considered relegating their mother to a witch, but I thought as an aunt she should most aptly be denominated Auntie Em, while my cousins held out to cast our grandmother as a good witch or as Em. I, however, uncharitably, sought to baptize my grandmother as the Wicked Witch of the West. Nevertheless, I was severely outvoted.

It amuses me now to think that we were plotting this in the rear of the car, while in the front and half of the middle seat sat the silent auditors, clearly within earshot. What this experience provided us, in any case, especially for me, however it was resolved, was a community, a band, and I felt gloriously embraced by a whole of many of whom I was an inextricably connected unit. I wanted everyone who saw us to assume we were a fine family of four children, two parents, and a grandmother, rather than to assign my three blue- or green-eyed, light-brown-haired cousins to the three similarly colored adults (though the gray-haired grandmother could also be an outlier), while my brown-eyed, brunette self looked more accurately like some tagalong orphan or the unique charge of the imperious elderly woman, as was the case.

We also played word games. My grandmother liked to think of rhymes. Thus, for one entertainment, we, the grandchildren, were obliged to devise rhymes for the names of animals she supplied us—"cat," "dog," "duck," pretty easy to think of words that sounded like those, "hat," "log," "luck"—but then she stumped us with "kangaroo." Many long minutes elapsed without anyone's positing a rhyme that worked. Then, our obviously multilingual grandmother exalted: "Dangereux!" And it was a dangereux landscape on which we strolled down the yellow brick road of boardwalk.

But we must hasten back to the South. We all loved the trip to Nags Head, to Blackbeard's hangout and Kitty Hawk, as well as those endless battlefields, haunted by the war of brother against brother. In Nags Head, at our hotel one evening all the children were to dress up as pirates. We all wore eye patches; someone must have tried to stumble with an improvised peg leg, and somehow I prevailed with permission to carry a twisted coat hanger as an arm hook, though I was disgruntled that my aunt and my grandmother, every time each encountered me, persisted in turning my hook increasingly inward and into an increasingly less viable hook. But missing limbs, missing eyes, what is the attraction of afflicted pirates that we all sought to render ourselves romantic and outlandish by virtue of a disability?

What my grandmother took back with her from that trip was a recipe for peanut-butter soup, which she and I enjoyed. Nonetheless, she could not quite match her recollection of the Virginia taste, try as she might. We experimented with endless variations until our insides must have been glued together from all the peanut butter.

When I was in the first grade or so, the nicest family one could imagine, and from the South of all mysterious places, moved into our neighborhood. Everyone on our block immediately cottoned to them. Rather than following the reserved dictates of Northern decorum, the members of the family called all the neighbor ladies, in proper Southern fashion, "Miss First Name"; the husbands were "Mr. First Name,'" but my grandmother, as she was in every other aspect of her life, was always and evidently satisfactorily to herself, "Mrs. Raab." At the time, I pondered that, though later I was pretty sure I had figured out why.

The family was deeply, generationally Southern, just arrived from below the Mason-Dixon Line. The family was the radiologist father from Louisiana, housewife mother from Alabama, Guy two years younger than I and born in Texas, and then Sam born right there in Johnstown.

One day I went to Guy's house after school to play, probably until my grandmother got home from a bridge game. When I came home, she asked me what we played.

"War."

"Oh, how did that go?"

"Well, first, Guy said, 'Charge.' So I thought we were at Penn Traffic. [My grandmother later regaled all her bridge friends with this misunderstanding.] Then he told me to stop trying to arrange the toy soldiers into families. He said just to call them all 'Joe.' Then he said I looked like a Scotsman."

"Was it because of your plaid skirt?" This gratified what my grandmother considered her prized Scotchness.

But, last, came the cropper.

"He told me we were shooting Yankees."

"Oh no, you can't do that. My grandfather, Captain Keller, was a Yankee."

Thus, the next time my grandmother had a bridge game, I reported to my general that the identity of our enemy needed to change.

Eagerly, when she picked me up, my grandmother inquired, "Who was the enemy today?"

"We were shooting Russians." And that, evidently, was fine. After all, this was at the height of the Cold War.

Many years later, after I had moved away, my cousin Fritz and I descended upon my grandmother at the Fourth of July. In preparation, our grandmother had bought for herself and her two grown grandchildren sparklers, which were legal in Pennsylvania then. It was a misty, rainy day (which makes me think it was 1976, one of the years that Johnstown was deluged and flooded) and for that reason we had to use the sparklers on the open-air front porch rather than going out into the yard to whirl and twirl the lighted sticks.

In my childhood, sparklers had always been the piece de resistance, and now I imagine that that must have been because they were my grandmother's delight, related to her sense of patriotism. I was not all that fond of them, because, frequently, the neighbor children, who always came running when Mrs. Raab bought sparklers, invariably dropped them into my often, by late afternoon, warm-water wading pool—also a feature that no one else had—where they singed ashy holes and made the pool leak.

Still, I remember the gun-powdery scent of the sparklers, the hiss as they were lit and burned down, and the radiant sparks shooting off in all directions. As Fritz and our grandmother and I twirled them in the air, she commanded us to write our names. Dutifully, he spelled out "F. R. I. T. Z. "; I created " L.A.U. R. A.," but I observed with increasing interest that my grandmother transcribed, silently, not "G. R. A. N. D. M. A.," not "M. A. R. J. O. R.I. E.," not even "M. O. T. H. E. R.," but "M. R. S. R. A. A. B."

And that makes me remember a time when I was in high school and became sick in the night. I thought that I should wake my grandmother to tell her. So I stood in the hall outside her open door and called, "Grandma! Grandma!"

No response.

"Mother! Mother!"

No answer.

"Marjorie! Marjorie!"

Nothing. Still I was ill. Still I needed her.

"Mrs. Raab!"

And she was out of bed in a flash.

Why? How did that become her identity? Not, I think, because of her sense of herself as a married woman. She never talked much about my grandfather. He was ten years older than she, a World War I veteran, an engineering graduate of the University of Pennsylvania, and later a highly successful executive at Bethlehem Steel, wounded once fairly seriously by a rock flung by striking steelworkers when he crossed a picket line to get to work, a mate who was picked out for her, the Vassar English major, by family friends. All that I recall she ever told me about him, besides his being a smoker, was that he remained a Lutheran all his life, never went to church with his Episcopal family and that he liked to go fishing but that she always hoped he would never catch anything because she did not want to have to clean the catch. This is something her child my aunt Marjie assured me was not the case, that she remembered her father's sitting on the back stoop patiently cleaning his fish. Ah, memories.

My grandmother also told me that her husband's dying words were "Ma... Ma...." She thought he was trying to say "Marjorie, I am sorry that I used the insurance to pave the alley and that you are going to have to go to work when I die right now at fifty-six from a bleeding ulcer." But she said his sister, Leone, thought he was trying to say, "Mother."

At any rate, my grandmother did have to go to work, which is perhaps why, years later, she always thought she was poor. Armed with her Vassar Bachelor of Arts degree in English, some graduate credits, and about a year of teaching experience, she met with the principal of the public school from which her son and my mother, her older daughter, had graduated and where my aunt Marjie was a junior. Teaching was all she knew to do. While she was in the principal's office, his phone rang. Calling was the principal of the next nearest high school, to find a lead on someone who could teach secondary-school English.

Thus my grandmother became a teacher and the chair of the English Department at Westmont Upper Yoder High School and yearbook advisor. Teaching was revealed to be her true vocation: Her students dedicated the 1952 annual to her, saying with high encomium, "Students leave her class not only with greatly increased knowledge of literature and grammar, but also with a better understanding of living in this world. Her patience and warm sense of humor will always be remembered by our class." Teaching high school was where she came into her own and found her identity as Mrs. Raab. Practically any time we went shopping, someone from the constellation of humanity known as Former Students would come up to her to ask how she was, to say how much she had taught them, and to see in what I was interested. "Why English, of course," she always said. And what was English for except to teach?

My grandmother taught high school English until the year she left midterm to travel to New Jersey to take care of me while my mother was hospitalized. Then, after my mother died, my grandmother took me along with her back to Johnstown, where she resumed teaching at Westmont while I stayed at home in the afternoons with a housekeeper after attending nursery school at Beth Zion Temple. But the times, circumstances were not as they had been before for her in the classroom.

"Discipline, "she said. "These students are not the same. They don't heed me as their older brothers and sisters did." Thus she quit in the middle of the year, again, and I was happy to get rid of the housekeeper, too, who had given me nothing but egg-salad sandwiches every day for lunch. To this day, I do not have good associations with egg-salad sandwiches. My grandmother did not go back to work, and consequently we were poor Appalachians.

My grandmother's battles to preserve the English language from the relentless assaults by ignorance and popular culture knew no bounds. Once in my youth when we were grocery shopping I nearly persuaded my grandmother, proud of her unsalted palate, bland to my taste buds, to purchase frozen pizza. I had almost won the dietary war that day until she discerned on the label the company's naïve claim to make good "pizza's." That was enough to scotch the purchase; she said, "No need to buy something and thereby encourage the riffraff." There would be no apostrophes in the plurals of our entrees.

Another of her linguistic taboos, which I hear committed incessantly, is to say, well-meaningly but, as my grandmother pointed out, truly nonsensically, that the reason for something is *because* of something else. As she said, "It is not the reason that is *because*, for if you think about that, that doesn't make any sense. The reason for something is *that* something else happened. To say 'the reason is because' introduces another level of causation." Well, that is probably not exactly what she said, probably too prolix for her more laconic and powerful style, but I hope it communicates her message. The reason that I am writing this memoir is that I want my grandmother to live.

Fortunately, I learned her lessons well. After my grandmother died, when my aunt and uncle and I were going through her desk, we found, in the small pile of papers that she had saved, copies of the two letters I had received in successive years telling me that I had been nominated for my institution's teacher-of-the-year award. I was glad I had sent those to her, though she had not commented much upon them at the time. Still, she, who was the antithesis of a packrat, having when I was away from home one summer, thrown out all my college notes and mementoes, had saved the letters that connected her profession with mine.

She must have been a wonderful teacher.

I heard about the time her students got into her classroom's locked closet somehow and stole the answer key to an objective test, true-false or multiple-choice, one of those. In reading the tests which her students turned in to her, she was surprised by the disproportionate distribution of good grades. Not stymied, she, in turn, surprised the class the next day with a test with the same questions, just rearranged. The grades resumed their appropriate allocation, and no other punishment had to be meted out.

Another time, one of her boys sat on the waist-high window sill of the second-floor classroom and announced, "I am going to jump out the window!"

She replied, "Well, be quick about it and don't make a mess. We have lessons to cover."

He slunk down and slid back to his chair.

Yet another young man, who in his youth, had had to have his teeth replaced, would open his mouth and roll his dentures around in there, defying his watchful teacher to laugh, but she assured me that she would not, externally, but was amused enough internally to report the story frequently.

Last of these is the story of the insufferable principal under whose incompetence she and her long-suffering colleagues labored. She told me, "He would slip into my classroom at the back, where the door was, and pretend to be checking the thermostat that was next to the door, but really he was checking on me and what was going on in the class. Then, one by one, a parade of the men teachers would come in, check the thermostat, and wink at me." Here is the other side of high-school teaching.

I was worried when I went to college because she had always proofread and edited my school papers. Somehow I figured out how to write, maybe because of her instructions earlier, her insistence upon correct English, not proper grammar. "Grammar is the rules," she preached. "You don't have good rules or bad rules. You have better or worse application of them. You don't have bad or good grammar. But you can have better or worse English." Because she preached a sensitivity to language, which is a large part of what she taught me about the mother tongue, what I took with me, bear in my heart, and trust to have instilled in my own students is that lesson, that ear, that ability to know and practice good English.

Do you know what Irish thin space is? Where the afterlife or the spirit world or the Platonic ideal or whatever else it might be called, even perhaps, the luminal world between wizards and muggles, sometimes touches, connects, and joins the everyday, matter-of-fact world of the here and now, across some filament, some veil, that dissolves for a moment, for a flash?

Once, this millennium, when I went on a pilgrimage to Ireland with a group of Unitarians, nearly all from North Carolina, we sat after dinner the first night introducing ourselves. I was the sole person from Georgia, but I had been on an Irish pilgrimage previously with the leaders of the group, though I did not know the others. A man from Florida was with us who did not know anyone else. Mr. Florida and Ms. Georgia, it turned out, had both grown up in Pennsylvania. In fact, further inquiry narrowed down that we had both grown up in western Pennsylvania, even in Johnstown.

Attentive, I said, "What high school did you attend? Maybe we know some of the same folks."

"I am much older than you; I was in high school in the early 1950s, so we likely didn't know the same people."

I persisted.

"Well, it was called Westmont Upper Yoder."

"That was the original name of my school. What year did you graduate?" I was almost bursting out of my chair.

He told me.

"The English teacher your senior year. . ."

". . . Was Mrs. Raab."

My grandmother. What he remembered of her, he said, was that she had let him write an essay on science fiction, about which she said she knew nothing, but about which she was interested to learn from him and that he appreciated that then and for many years thereafter. A Former Student. I appreciated what she had done and what he remembered too. I felt my grandmother's spirit with us, perhaps blessing this unexpected connection. It was an instance of an Irish thin space, when there was a brief contingency, a linkage across time and space.

Many waters cannot quench love.

A singular lesson concerning the facts of life that my grandmother was willing to impart to me occurred when I was about to be launched off to summer camp. She told me about menstruation and she observed, sitting on the lid of the toilet while I was in the bathtub, that I might hear some of the older girls at camp talking about the curse or their monthlies, and I might wonder and out of ignorance ask impertinent questions. One thing her lesson neglected to tell me was of the periodicity of the flux, so I thought all over the world, all women were constantly and endlessly menstruating. The reality was, in a way, a relief. But the important lesson was not to speak out of ignorance but rather from an informed perspective.

As one might expect, my grandmother did not want to give me the other, larger story of the origin of life, of sex. We had just two conversations on that subject. When the movie *Lawrence of Arabia* came to town, she took me to see it. I was most struck by a comment early on when one character said to another something to the effect, "You know that his parents were never married."

"What?" I nudged my grandmother. "How can that be?"

"Shhh. I'll tell you later when we get home," she whispered, obviously hoping I would forget.

Something like that a child is not likely to forget, though it was not until after I had gone to bed that I remembered the incident. Then, I got out of bed, opened my bedroom door a crack, to remind her, reading in the living room, to tell me how an unmarried couple could have a baby.

Obviously, she saw an opportunity here. "That is what happens when girls let boys get too familiar with them."

What familiar? Hence, I was not sure from thence on and for some time to come what degree of familiarity was within permissible range. What were the boundaries? Was it safe to say hello? Could I ask how the boy or boys were? Maybe that was the limit. But no farther.

The next opportunity for a further chapter in my sexual education came when my grandmother and cousin Connie and I shared a hotel/motel room with its two double beds as we always did, on one of our vacation trips. Connie always wanted to share a bed with me so my grandmother could have a bed to herself, while my grandmother thought she and I should sleep together so that Connie, for some reason, could have the spare bed. Nonetheless, that prospect horrified me because the few times we arranged ourselves that way I lay awake most of the night afraid that, if I fell asleep, I would kick my grandmother, killing her. For me, the ideal distribution, since they were both so determined to share a bed, was for the two of them to sleep together so that I could have the solitary bed. When I kept losing the argument every evening, I finally announced, "When I am grown up and married," which to my mind were equivalent states of being independent, "I shall have a bed to myself."

To that, Connie decisively retorted, "Then you won't have any children." My grandmother smiled blissfully at that reply. Now that was a pickle to contemplate. It led to me to consider the sleeping arrangements of all the married couples I knew, but the answer did not make me any more sexually enlightened. As for any more information, never mind.

My cousin Fritz was very concerned that I would not learn about the birds and the bees correctly. He asked his mother, my aunt Marjie, to volunteer to my grandmother that she, my aunt, would inform me properly, but Aunt Marjie was told, in effect, never mind. Thus, one hot summer day, Fritz and I took folding lawn chairs to the far end of the backyard next to a boundary wall of tall, overgrown forsythia bushes, and he, who is twenty months my junior, set me straight. Later, we heard that the others wondered what on earth we were so earnestly talking about there at the back of the yard, but we never said, and I do not know whether Aunt Marjie or anyone else ever figured it out.

Another time, when Fritz and I were many years older, he and I came to visit my grandmother at the same time, just as we had that time we spelled our names with sparklers. The three of us went out to dinner, with me driving her aging, monstrous, brilliant buttery American Motors Ambassador, which succeeded the trusty Chevy Nova. As we were heading home up what is called Easy Grade, a two-lane road circling up and around the hillside that separates Westmont borough where Sunshine Avenue is, and Johnstown, in that flood-prone valley, I became aware that the old car was laboring. I did not want to panic my passengers, but I did not know what to do. There was no shoulder as we rounded up the hillside, just steep, virtually perpendicular, rocky hillside on one side and straight descent to the valley on the other. "Come on, car; come on, car," I silently coaxed, while Fritz and our grandmother prattled on.

As we got to the top of the hill, where suddenly all is comparably level, stretching to the right toward the open land of Grandview Cemetery, on the other side, the pristine wide lawns of Ye Olde Country Club of Bethlehem Steel, and ahead of us the grounds of the Beth Zion Temple, the car coughed, sputtered, and died as billows of ominous smoke wafted from it.

"Get out! Get out!" I shouted.

Fritz was out of the backseat like a jackrabbit. My grandmother seemed unable to unhook her seatbelt. I ran around to the passenger door to extricate her.

At the same time, a car that had been behind us came to a stop. A woman got out. "Do you know what the matter is?"

No, I did not. None of us did.

"I could tell you were in trouble coming up Easy Grade. I'll go get help for you." And she was gone. And we never knew who our angel was.

Eventually, a tow truck from a local garage appeared. The mechanic attached the great yellow behemoth to the tow, and instructed Fritz, our grandmother, and me to hop in the seat alongside him. My grandmother climbed in first, then I, then Fritz. We were sandwiched together tightly, and we were starting emotionally to come down from the scare.

My grandmother poked my side. "Look how I am sitting," she stage whispered.

I looked over. She had positioned herself so that she was athwart the gearshift. The poor driver had to reach between her legs to shift gears.

What could I say? What could I do? I just nudged Fritz to point out this arrangement, and he and I snickered the whole way home.

iii. Avocations

Besides having been an English teacher and, therefore, by her definition, devoted to the theatre and to Shakespeare, my grandmother had an avocation as an actress. She had performed in community-theatre productions, directed by another Vassar graduate, while her children were growing up, but there were fewer opportunities when I came along. Her last major role was as Kent, the loyal aide-de-camp, in *King Lear*. As a child with a strict early bedtime, I did not get to see the evening-only performances, but I was fascinated by the aluminum-foil, faux-armor costume that hung outside the hall-closet door of our house until show time. When she was not in the room, I would inspect it, though its rustling always gave me away. And she who must always be obeyed was not pleased. But the armor tantalized me. I had never seen such a good use of aluminum foil. And I imagine my grandmother was grand indeed, decked out in it.

Later, when I was given roles in two Christmas plays—as Mary in the church pageant and as Santa Claus with my Girl Scout troop—my grandmother endlessly rehearsed my lines with me, over and over and over so that I would be line perfect, intoning appropriately and in character. I profited from her thespian experience and knowledge, but I never took to the stage as she might have wished.

Like the young women of Jane Austen's time and novels, I was reared to be accomplished or at least exposed to many of the other arts as my grandmother defined them. She had had her acting; I too had to have an avocation or avocations as an important constituent element in my preparation for adulthood under her tutelage. I was taken to the local YWCA for French and swimming lessons at various points. But, first I was subjected to ballet lessons, which lasted until one inauspicious day, no doubt when I was gracefully executing a pirouette, when I threw up all over the studio floor. After being unceremoniously bustled away on that occasion, I was relieved not to return to the scene of my disgrace, terminating my rise toward prima-donna-hood.

Next, twice, my grandmother tried tap dancing lessons for me with different teachers and studios, but to no avail. In all three of these dance undertakings, I was enrolled in a class that included a close family friend, a young girl my own age, who enjoyed the classes but always companionably quit when I inevitably did. Thus, it was not for lack of society that I failed. Rather, I must lack the requisite desire to perform physically and publicly necessary to become a dancer, while my friend went on to great triumph as a cheerleader.

The experiment with tap dancing had a singularly familial aspect. In her youth, my mother Lydia and her siblings, experiencing their own avocational apprenticeships under the instigation of their mother, had taken tap dancing in the early thirties from a very young and as yet undiscovered Gene Kelly, who would come to Johnstown from his home in Pittsburgh on Saturdays to teach tap. Years later, my mother wrote to him to congratulate him on some film or other, saying in evidently characteristic humility something to the effect of "naturally you don't remember me from my dancing lessons from you in Johnstown," and been most surprised and gratified to receive a postcard from the movie star himself that said, definitively, "Oh, yes, Lydia, I do indeed remember you and your big blue eyes," which was apparently her greatest distinguishing feature; though since she died when I was a year old, I do not recall her face other than from images in black-and-white snapshots. But I yet possess the postcard!

Nonetheless, my grandmother was not done with me yet. For a year or two, she contracted with a teacher at my elementary school, not one of mine, who was, like me, left-handed, for penmanship lessons in ease and legibility. My grandmother had known children whose dominant hand had been dictatorially switched from left to right and who had suffered anxieties as a result. She did not wish that for me. However, as my own students would surely later testify, those lessons did not take. I rarely write legibly, but I am not anxious.

For several years I suffered through ice-skating lessons. Two neighbor girls took to the ice quite capably, and I rode with them as their mother drove us down Easy Grade on cold, wintry nights to the War Memorial, a stolid edifice erected to memorialize World War II, the site of the flood-memorial dinners my grandmother and I had attended, which also sheltered the indoor skating rink where Johnstown's professional hockey team hosted its competitions. The name of the site of the rink frequently occasioned the pun that my grandmother enjoyed on the rare occasions that the weather was temperate enough for her to drive us, and she would sit in the stands to watch and wait: "There is nothing warm at all about the so-called Warm Emorial." I managed to pass two figure-skating proficiency tests, but I did not like skating any more than I had been fond of dancing, though I endured several winters of it. Johnstown's hockey team did better than I because years later Paul Newman came to town to film *Slapshot*, about small-town ice hockey and its ice-skating community, including in the movie people whom I had known at the rink. But their world was not the world for me. Once more, I might have been touched by a Hollywood star, but I bowed out too soon.

Like Jane Austen's young women of Regency England and according to my grandmother, music needed to be an important constituent element of my finishing. In elementary school I very briefly bore up under the indignities of group clarinet lessons from the high-school band-leader who descended through the grades to teach as part of his professional assignments. I was foreordained to play clarinet because it had been my mother's instrument—I even had to play on the very same nickel-plated device. I hated it, and it probably hated my half-hearted, unpracticed attempts to wrench music out of it. Moreover, when all my clarinet-playing colleagues, my erstwhile skating neighbors, graduated to more solid, more artistic-looking, fatter and more successful-appearing ebony apparati, I was still stuck with the metal tube, because, of course, according to my grandmother, "if it was good enough for your mother . . ." I did not care for the mortification I felt at my low-class stick, and I got out of this exercise as swiftly as I could, to the tunes of my father and grandmother bewailing my lack of a developing ear.

That no doubt proved the case when the cultural despair of baby-boomer parents hit with the Beatles' invasion. For me, I was passionate to play guitar. I suppose my caretakers reasoned that it was at least a means to get me to music lessons. My father brought me a nice amateurs' model with metal strings, so that I might begin private lessons in classical guitar. But that was not what I wanted to play. This time, when the instructor urged an instrumental upgrade, to a lovely Yamaha with nylon strings—thus to be more euphoniously strummed, not plucked cacophonously with a pick—I was in place to make beautiful sounds. This time I was granted the promotion to a superior instrument. Predictably, I hated the new guitar no less than the old one or than the clarinet. This teacher was overworked, having thirty-minute, back-to-back sessions on Saturdays with recalcitrant, uninspired students. Once, I looked over at him, sitting next to me, to discover that he was fast asleep. I did not blame him.

I so loathed practicing that I devised a system to avoid learning my lessons. I was supposed to master three new chords for each assignment and then to play some pages' worth of rotations of them, written out in musical notation. However, the music was just a pattern of the three new chords. Industriously, I translated the sequences from music to numbers, assigning "1," "2," and "3" to the new chords, and Saturday mornings before my lesson, at the branch of the public library several doors down from where the music teacher held court, where my grandmother volunteered at the circulation desk, I sat at a table and memorized the sequence. Then, at my class, I just played the sequence, which I could have done, in emulation of my teacher, with my eyes closed—"1," "2, "3," "1," "2," "3," "3," "2," "1," "3," "2," "3," "1," "1,"2," whatever, ad infinitum. Now I think, surely it would have been easier to practice. But the joy was in the rebellion, for which, perhaps, I had been reared to strive.

My grandmother was very angry at my resistance to practicing either clarinet or guitar in the proper ways, at home, daily, for a minimum of thirty minutes—even twenty minutes which the guitar teacher had dangled once as a peace offering. We quarreled magisterially over it. One occasion, she even brandished a hairbrush as if to hit me. She may or may not have made contact, but what we both remembered was that the hairbrush splintered, and she was injured, bleeding as a result.

As I was growing up, growing into the English major and professor I became, my grandmother had another mission for me, which probably was connected to the dancing lessons and the clarinet. I knew that the parents of my friends praised and encouraged high grades, but my grandmother would look at my report cards, especially from high school, and say, "You don't have to get all A's. Your mother didn't get all A's. And your mother had a lot of friends. All you ever want to do is to read." In the summers she would say, "Why don't you invite some of your school friends over?" What I came to realize was that my father and grandmother hoped to make me into a new, resurrected version of my mother, dead before her time. Alas, I was turning into the English major that my grandmother had been.

Aside from the incident of the hairbrush, the only other punishment that I recall having been administered at the hand of my grandmother was when I was very young. She burned in a raging fire in our fireplace, as I recollect, flaming orange and red and terrible in its power, my paper dolls before they were even all cut out. I do not recall the offense that I had allegedly perpetrated that necessitated the conflagration of my paper-doll tribe; years later I remember my grandmother saying, "Do you want me to buy you paper dolls now? I am sick unto death of hearing about these paper dolls I am supposed to have burned up."

Then at last in the course of the efforts to prepare me for my adulthood my grandmother had an inspiration that satisfied both of us, though in unsuspected ways I later learned. She would subject me to art lessons. I had three different art teachers over the course of several years, and I loved the experiences. Pastels and watercolors, acrylics and oil, still life and landscape, I adored the classes and the execution. It was great fun. I did not have any particular talent, but it was surely a positive contribution to my rearing, to my maturation, to have attempted to express myself visually, as opposed to physically on the ice or the dance-floor.

Years later when my aunt and I sorted through my grandmother's possessions after her death, we found a set of watercolor paints that my grandmother had had. She had ostensibly bought them, one of us remembered, as a gift for someone, but then she had saved them for herself, it was apparent, for they had been used. Sadly, no traces of her illustrations remained. It was especially poignant for both my aunt and me, for we had both had art lessons at my grandmother's encouragement, and the framed paintings throughout my grandmother's house on Sunshine Avenue were those that had been crafted by my aunt and me. Vicariously, perhaps, we had gotten to do what she would have liked to have done. Thus, my lessons and those of my aunt were a way of fulfilling her secret desires, it seems. I am sorry I was not better for her.

One of the reasons that it is extraordinary that my grandmother saved the watercolor set is that she was, as I have shown, the anti-packrat. She did not save anything, it seemed. Spring cleaning must have been her favorite activity of year, I often thought, and I always tried to make myself scarce during the upheaval. Now it seems apparent that that was one of her ways of dealing with all her losses. She did not choose to be sentimental, and she did not want to be surrounded by bric-a-brac, tchotchkes, and any incidental items that might have been invested with emotional values that would silently raise specters of her losses, causing her painful memories of what was gone.

Through my childhood, my grandmother had insisted, whenever the local chapter of the AAUW, of which she was a proud member, held its annual used book sale, which was one of my favorite events, that I must donate books in order to make room for my purchases. Such agony. Such exquisite choices. I felt that my books were the external pictures of the internal landscape of my mind and myself, so how could I discard part of my identity? But my grandmother was obdurate. So, to get even with her one year, on the top of small pile of very old books I deigned to give away, was a collection of light-blue-covered children's stories, bound with brighter blue spines, about youngsters around the world, illustrated with black-and-white photographs, and written by Madeline Brandeis.

"These were your mother's. You want to give them away?"

I could be stubborn too. Of course, I am sure my grandmother knew I was doing this out of resistance. But she sighed and let me do it. And I have ever since regretted it, for I remember that my mother had carefully inscribed her name and applied her address labels in the fronts of all of those volumes. It is hard now for me to believe that I could have been so obstinate and so foolish. My grandmother allowed me to learn that lesson; she did not overrule my immaturity. Somewhere, I hope another child has enjoyed those books and appreciated them more than I did.

My grandmother was a prodigious lover of animals, and here she did express herself. One early morning, she roused me to see a deer in our suburban backyard on Sunshine Avenue. As mysteriously as it had appeared, it vanished, but I can still remember its motionless solitude, watching us from far down our deep backyard as we, breathlessly, watched it until we turned away and it was gone.

We always had multitudes of rabbits and birds and moles and chipmunks to watch and hummingbirds for which my grandmother installed a trellis of honeysuckle on the wall of the back porch. Silently, we would watch these miniature hoverers. And any time a strange bird would appear in our yard, my grandmother would tell me to get out our bird guide so we might identify it, among the robins, cardinals, blue jays, starlings, galore which we generally witnessed.

My grandmother was exceedingly excited when the house next door, which was on the corner and had a big yard surrounded by a tall hedge on three sides and pine trees on our side, was bought from the Haddocks (and later sold to the Herrons, while on the other side our neighbors were the Hahns—German for rabbit). The new owner was a Syrian Orthodox church a couple miles away, and the house would be its rectory. Two priests moved in, my grandmother discovered, but what most impressed her was their St. Bernard or some other gigantic, hairy canine whose name she swiftly and somehow definitively ascertained was Humphrey. Another H.

"Come over to meet Humphrey," she would urge me.

"No, I don't want to meet a dog."

"He's lonely, outside all day long until the priests come home."

"How do you know he's lonely?"

"Wouldn't you be?"

"No, I just want to be left alone."

My grandmother was forever, in fact, as I have said, urging me to call my friends from school in the summer to get together, but all I wanted to do was to read. She would say, "Go outside, get some sunlight, talk to Humphrey."

Dutifully, I would go outside with a lawn chair and a book and sit under our apple tree. Alone. Reading English classics, imagining far-flung worlds and times away from Johnstown, hemmed in by its oppressive mountains.

In the meantime, my grandmother would take Humphrey bones from roasts of beef and lamb. Lots of lamb. My cousins told me that they used to joke about coming to visit Grandma and Laura—which always made me think that I was in lieu of Grandpa and that there was a way in which my cousins were my grandchildren—and having to eat lamb patties. They look like hamburgers until tasted when one discovered the deception. Lamb in any form is not a favored children's treat. Thus, my cousins reminisced about going to visit Grandma and Laura, having to eat lamb patties and imbibe Alka-Seltzer-like flavored Fizzies. These she bought especially for the grandchildren, who universally disdained them once they had dissolved. The elation was in the dissolution. Still, for herself, our grandmother venerated lamb. It was the prince of meats as far as she was concerned, and her preferred method of cooking was rendering meat well-done, while saving the bones for anyone who had a dog. Thus, Humphrey was surely in doggy heaven to live next door to us.

Nonetheless, I thoroughly disapproved of her intervention in the neighbors' affairs, manifested by taking old bones to Humphrey, whom I refused to engage.

When I first came to live with my grandmother, she had had a short-haired black cat named "Tarzi," short for Tarzan. I have only dim recollections of him, prowling the kitchen floor, but I think his name was certainly noble.

For four years we had the best cat, whose name was Fluffy. He was big, long-haired, and all black, except for one white whisker. He had blue eyes as a kitten, but then they changed to yellow, wise, shrewd, all-seeing orbs. He loved my grandmother, who fed him. Me, he tolerated, which was probably smart on his part. He liked to sleep in the empty bathtub, though I tried once to interest him in it when it was full of water, the result of which no doubt contributed to his less than amiable feelings toward me. Well, what can I say in my defense? Many waters cannot quench love, yes?

Fluffy was sweet-tempered and nearly never spoke. Though once he cried, and I rushed and saved him and thus may well have been in his good graces for a while. It happened this way:

On the other side of Humphrey's yard from us was the very busy, two-lane county route of Goucher Street. Hence, my grandmother decreed that Fluffy did not have free-ranging privileges. Instead, she bought five or six dog leashes, which she attached end-to-end to his collar, at one end, and, as long as he was small, at the other end to an ancient cast-iron, historically genuine clothes-pressing iron she had. It had been her grandmother's or that of someone even longer ago than that, and it was shaped just like the implement that we know that presses clothes, but it was solid and heavy, pre-electrical. My grandmother would take Fluffy outside, where he had quite a circuit he could navigate, kept confined within the bounds of the dog-leashed iron. However, as he got older, bigger, and stronger, he could drag that iron across quite a bit of the expanse of the yard. Until one day, when I was reading, of course, in the sunroom at the back of the house, I heard him crying. I dashed out to liberate him from near-certain hanging. The poor cat had twisted all his leashes around the lower branches of the forsythia bushes that lined the back of the yard, leaving him suspended by the neck in midair. Ultimately, Fluffy was okay, but that was the end of his bondage to the iron.

As an alternative, my grandmother attached Fluffy's train of leashes to the clothesline-pole. But then sometimes he would run around and around and around that, diminishing his mobility, which was bad enough, until one dire emergency when I was startled to see a blue jay dive-bombing him. Again I rushed from my book to free Fluffy. I reacted probably at the same time that he did, and both of us scared off the vicious avian.

In consequence of that failed venture, then, either my grandmother or I would take Fluffy for walks around the yard with merely the length of one or two leashes attached. Or mostly my grandmother would do that. I was not as accommodating or generous with my time. Truly, I am sorry now. For surely what would not be more pleasant than to linger through a yard, stopping to sniff at the shrubbery, to pause before a flight of a bird overhead, to listen to the wind, to stalk a brazen chipmunk, to enjoy the warm sun on a mellow afternoon?

Nonetheless, such joys were not sufficient unto Fluffy, for he tried mightily to escape the house every time anyone came to the door. Not for him the leash-upon-leash indignity. Most of the time he was restrained by someone, usually me, grabbing him before he got away. Our friends and family had to learn to ease themselves practically sideways through the doorway, with the door barely ajar, to keep Fluffy from escaping. Still, occasionally he did get out. Thereupon, dashing out of the house, Fluffy would scamper up one of the pine trees next door where he would station himself, perched on a branch high above us, just assessing a larger world than he was accustomed to. I would have to get out our long extension ladder and climb up, up, up, as far as I could go, holding out my arms over my head toward his roost, for minutes, a quarter of an hour, once nearly an entire hour, or so, it least it seemed, until he would descend into my arms, purring, and I would maneuver him and me down to earth and security. But, oh, he was at it again, the next time someone came to the door.

It was heart-breaking when at just four years of age he developed kidney disease. The veterinarian thought he might be able to save Fluffy, but Fluffy's suffering was terrible. My grandmother had brought his litter box upstairs from the basement for his convenience, and he either did not see it or did not like its relocation because early one morning I heard him crying his way down the basement stairs. I ran again to his aid, brought him upstairs, and deposited him in the box in its new location. However, that arrangement merely lasted for a few hours while I was at school. He was clearly dying. While I was at school, my grandmother took him one last time to the vet. And the deed was done.

Afterwards, sometime after I had cried though my stoical grandmother had not, at least in my presence, I asked if we could get another cat. "No. It is too sad when they die. I can't go through any more losses," she said. How could I argue with that? She had lost her parents, her husband, and her oldest child in a brief passage of time. No more losses indeed. Many waters.

iv. The Spiritual Life

Memorial Day was an exceptional day in Johnstown. Of course, it had its own particular merits in commemoration of the war dead from its origins as the Civil War Decoration day. But also, in Johnstown, the Great Flood of 1889 occurred on the day after the calendar's Memorial Day—that is, not the arbitrary, later congressionally imposed Monday holiday—but on May 31st, therefore underscoring a juxtaposition with the holiday. A third reason for holiday's specialness was that it generally coincided with a time that leftover flowers intended for Mother's Day could be had at cut-rate prices, so my penurious grandmother could buy geraniums—one white, four red—for us to plant at graves at Grandview Cemetery.

Grandview was built on the Westmont hillside overlooking Johnstown, as its name suggests, and there was one place where a splendid vista opened up between the trees, of the river wending beside the sprawling, gray, long low expanse of the Bethlehem Steel plant far below. Accordingly, when we went to Grandview, we would stop to admire the splendor, the vision of what had rebuilt Johnstown after the devastation of the Great Flood, that monolithic capitalistic enterprise, seemingly stalwart for the ages. Inevitably, of course, I would take pictures, which invariably when developed, were only of trees.

The cemetery itself had its marvels. I remember when the milestone was passed that there were more dead people planted in Grandview, a monumental plantation of the dead — fifty thousand? Sixty thousand? Seventy thousand?—than alive in the city. Amid Grandview's marvels is a circle of small rounded tombstones and graves surrounding a pillar with a statue of a Yankee soldier atop it to designate the interment of Civil War casualties, ironically similar to the statues of Confederate soldiers that I have seen in many Southern towns today.

In Grandview, too, there is the plain of seven hundred seventy-seven bodies of the unidentified victims of the Great Flood, including, presumably, that of my great-great aunt, lined up behind a tall monument I have mentioned before on which stands a carved angel asking us to pause and pray before the lost.

Also, there are many sepulchers, private chapels, spread over the rolling hills and valleys of this vast metropolis of the dead, amid the rows and rows of smaller tombstones, granite, impervious, stolid among the even, regular mounds rising up in the freshly mown lawns. We drove by sections of Jewish graves, marked by Hebrew inscriptions; Orthodox Christian graves, with photographs of the departed affixed to the tombstones beside Cyrillic letters; there was a rose-colored pavilion, large enough for one to stand in or sit on a bench beneath its roof, where it announced, "THE TEMPLE OF LOVE." That always makes me think of William Blake's poem of "The Garden of Love," in which the poet writes of a garden "filled with graves, /And tombstones where flowers should be." Strangely, perhaps, in keeping with the mournful tone of Blake's poem, we never saw anyone sitting in Grandview's temple, standing there, resting there, and heeding its blessing. It seemed neglected, resistant to the living human world as much of the cemetery always seemed. Yet it was always very peaceful there surrounded by graves, calling out silently for pause, for recollection, for time.

We would drive the narrow, well-paved lanes, occasionally but infrequently seeing other cars, also driving slowly or parked near where someone, at a distance, could be sighted bent over a grave, tending, standing, or maybe kneeling beside it.

Once I spotted the tombstone of some people my grandmother knew who had not yet died. I was stunned. It was as if, it seemed to me, these people were inviting death, asking for it. But my grandmother was nonplused. "They are saving their children the expense and worry of getting a tombstone when the time comes. For it will come. And sooner rather than later."

And thus my grandmother drove us serenely, silently, meditatively through the cemetery over and around and through, looking for our highpoints, looking for graves of people she had known, looking at the graves of thousands of strangers, thousands now united in death for eternity in Grandview Cemetery. Grandview was surely a central spot of my childhood, of my grandmother's life. It represented a connection, a nexus, to those who had died, perhaps a threshold to wherever they now dwelt. It was yet another of the landscapes we explored by car from which I might learn about this world, pointing to the next, and for my grandmother, I suspect, to entertain memories.

Usually, though, these tours followed the execution of our principal business at the cemetery. First, right inside the cemetery's gate, we parked and walked, carrying three of the geraniums we had brought, along with a trowel and a bucket of water, filled from one of the street-side pumps. Our destination was three identical, simple, small, light-colored tablets of granite, denoting three mounds that hid graves, where her parents and elder brother of one day's life lay. There she planted two red geraniums and the single white one. For sixty, seventy years, every year, the unnamed baby boy received his white geranium.

Like me, my grandmother had been an only child. These were the graves of her original nuclear family. She would kneel to plant the flowers, never asking or instructing me to help. Digging out the remnants if any of last year's plants, excavating holes for this year's, cleaning around the grave, inserting the new flower, and then covering the hole and pouring some water on the flower. There. Done for another year.

Then, back in the car, traveling more deeply into the cemetery, we eased slowly toward a large, overbearing gray stone, deliberately ragged-looking, clearly shaped to be rough, as if age and time could not hasten swiftly enough to make their changes, labeled "Heslop." Here she would slow and stop. We were in sight of the Civil War section, but that was not our destination.

Rather down an aisle of grass of maybe half a city block in distance between rows of graves, being careful not to step on any, we paced till coming to an intersection of paths and the Raab corner, two rows of graves. In front, two graves (and two empty spaces for new graves at some undefined time in the future) were marked by low, squared, gray tombstones that sloped back slightly to make it easier, I suppose, to read boxed inscriptions. In the back, behind these graves, reared one taller double grave marker, designating the mounds where my grandmother's in-laws rested, but she did not attend to them; they were the responsibility of her sister-in-law Aunt Leone, her husband's only sibling. But in front, nearest the path, there was room for one grave, not yet in use; next was a grave; then a space—""This is where I'll be buried," she told me—then her husband's grave, that of my grandfather, with a stand holding a small American flag to mark him as a veteran of World War I. But I paid little heed to that grave. It was the first one, next to the empty space, about which I cared.

The tablet had three rows of words and numbers. "Lydia Elizabeth Raab Dabundo," it read at the top. Below that was inscribed, "July 13, 1924–October 26, 1954." Below that were the words, "Infant Daughter," and at the bottom of the entire inscription: "October 26, 1954." The unnamed infant daughter did not even live to have a name or to earn two dates and to have a life contained by the dash between the two dates. She died before she was born, stillborn. All of her life, all of her identity, is consumed in the one single date, and she is nameless but yet remembered. Certainly, I felt all through my childhood the ghost of her presence; I felt that I was not an only child but that I had an angel sister who shared my family with me. Perhaps my grandmother felt that way about her older brother, though I am not sure we ever spoke of the matter. Sometimes in my mind, my grandmother's brother merged with my sister, he who lived one day merging with her who had no life at all except what the afterlife gave her now in Grandview, Pennsylvania, though she lived and died, her life in the womb, that is, while my mother was pregnant in New Jersey. Holy innocents, both of them. My dead sister had not had any life in Pennsylvania whatsoever though she now was surrounded for eternity by the Pennsylvania soil and dead of her maternal heredity, buried in the same grave with her mother. She was united with our mother. For that reunion, I would have to wait.

"Is the empty place next to my mother's grave where my father will be buried?" I asked my grandmother once.

"Oh, I doubt that he wants to be buried here, though I guess he could be if he chose. But why would he want to be buried here? I am sure he would rather be buried in New Jersey with his people." My grandmother threw that comment off as if my mother were not my father's people. But he had obviously consented to my mother's interment here in Johnstown, surrounded by Raabs, reunited with her parents and one set of grandparents for time everlasting.

My grandmother would plant the two remaining geraniums here for her husband and her elder daughter. "When you die, will someone plant geraniums here for you and for the others?" I wondered.

"That will be your job. Or Uncle Harry's. Or Aunt Marjie's. Someone will do it. That is what the living do. They keep the memories alive."

But what could I remember of my mother? Just a tombstone. And a sister who had never lived. No one ever spoke to me of my mother. Her death had been too sudden, out of time, out of place. She was a statistic, in some way, one of the last victims of one of the last summers that polio struck America before the Salk vaccine offered salvation.

"She baked your first birthday cake and said she wasn't feeling well," my grandmother told me.

So she became sick on my birthday. I knew what that meant. Her death was my fault.

And she lived two more months, difficult times, in a small New Jersey hospital, an adult, pregnant, where, it seemed, it was easier for children to be tended than an expectant adult. She made colorful yarn squares which my grandmother stitched together years later to become a blanket for me, holding me as my mother's hands had held the squares. But that was not sufficient therapy for my hospitalized mother, who developed the pulmonary embolism that dispatched her.

"If she had lived," my grandmother mused, "She might have had to use a wheelchair."

"So you think she was better off to have died?"

"Perhaps. Don't you think so?" My grandmother had a way of turning her statements into questions like that, positioning me to be the one to make the judgment.

I could not answer that, for even if my mother had been wheelchair-bound, at least she would have been alive, and I could have known her, I thought, but I decided that that was selfish thinking. Who was I to insist on a life for her as an invalid when now she could live with the angels, which I knew she was doing, watching over her mother and me?

"When you graduated from high school," my grandmother told me, some years later, "I had the feeling that your mother was with me, telling me that it was all right, that she was pleased with how I had reared her daughter."

Yet to me that seemed too early, when I was just eighteen, for someone to say that it was all right, as if my life were over before it had even begun. Or so it seemed at the time. Yet now I know that that time with my grandmother was surely precious. Death and life and life and death as experienced at the cemetery were hallowed, special, and integrated into daily life, as I learned in the church, the love of which my grandmother bequeathed to me by her example and practice every Sunday. She did not talk about faith much, but she did once say to me, "What if the Second Coming is as humble as the first? What if it is not recognized then? What if it has already happened?" I did not want to contemplate these questions; I do not know if she did. She also took to heart the gospel reading for Ash Wednesday in which Christ warns, "'Beware of practicing your piety before others in order to be seen by them; for then you have no reward from your Father in heaven.'" He even continues to stipulate that one should wash one's face in order to maintain that privacy (Matt. 6: 1–5, 16 [NRSV]). Thus, my grandmother said, "Wash the ashen cross from your forehead before you venture out into public."

Although I never questioned the appropriateness of the place of my baptism while I was growing up, I now think it strange that my parents brought me all the way from New Jersey when I was just two months old to be baptized at St. Mark's. They were not planning to return to Johnstown to live, especially since my father's employer was the Philadelphia Electric Company. Moreover, none of my eight first cousins on my mother's side were so transported from afar to join Christ's church in Johnstown, though all were baptized in Episcopal churches where they were then living. Paradoxically, since a year after my own baptism I came to live with my grandmother and to grow up in that church, it always seemed fitting that I had been baptized there, in the same church in which my mother and grandmother had been baptized, in which my parents and one set of grandparents had been married, and where the funerals were held for a series of three maternal ancestors, my mother, my grandmother, and her mother. St. Mark's was truly the church of my family and my grandmother's church. Family bonds can embrace across generations. For us, St. Mark's was the central repository of our life in faith, another marker, like Grandview, of what life infinitely and eternally promises and means, another and different doorway to a very real, to my grandmother, spiritual realm, the place where the altar inscription very simply affirmed, "Many waters cannot quench love."

I remember my grandmother kneeling very still, with her eyes closed, resting back on the seat behind her, during those interminable, nearly ten pages from 76 to 84 of the consecration of the communion service according to the 1928 Book of Common Prayer. I used to kneel there, too, though obviously with my eyes wide open, counting down the pages as the priest intoned the prayers and blessings, wishing the church would catch on fire or that something extraordinary might happen before my eyes and enable an escape, before finally we would troop from our pew in the second row up to the altar, to receive the sacred elements. Then, we would return to our seats, and I at least would have the diversion of watching the rest of the congregation make its way, person by person, up to the altar and then back to their seats. Whatever internal extraordinary event happened at that altar was not for me to know or experience, in my youth at least.

When I think of church, I remember my grandmother singing. She did not have a very good voice, and neither do I, so that I suppose people who sit around me now rather wish I would keep quiet, if not shut up. However, I did not wish that my grandmother kept quiet. In fact, there are hymns still in our revised hymnal, to which, if I close my eyes, I can yet hear her voice, especially: "When morning gilds the skies, / My heart awaking cries, /May Jesus Christ be praised."

When I was growing up, we had communion just once a month. In the late 1970s, though, the revision of the Book of Common Prayer shortened the communion service and revised the language of the Eucharist to involve the congregation so that the service was not so much entirely the priest's show. Now the priest turned around from the altar to face the congregation. Always, my grandmother and I went to church every Sunday, for Morning Prayer most Sundays, as long as the weather held, with our female heads hatted, in accordance with St. Paul's instructions. Of course, as I have said, my grandmother would not drive in the bad weather, snow or ice, no matter how gradual the incline of Easy Grade, no matter how heavy and solid the Packard or the Nova or the Ambassador, no matter how well armed with snow tires the car might have been. She was not going to venture dangerously from Westmont to Johnstown, to the only Episcopal Church in all of Cambria County, full of steel mills and coal mines, clearly not a part of the nation that had lured very many Anglicans. In fact, we were of that faith because her father, an Anglican, had come to Johnstown from Canada to be an executive at the U.S. Steel plant, also in Johnstown, like Bethlehem Steel's, but smaller.

Thereby, in cold, wintry western Pennsylvania, it was important to keep apprised of the conditions outside in order to know how much to bundle up in order to set forth or even if we were to set forth. We had a thermometer affixed to the exterior of the house on Sunshine Avenue, visible to be read from a window in the living room. One time my grandmother said that before we went out we needed to see what Arthur said.

"Arthur?" I exclaimed. My grandmother always said she did not have a very good memory for names, and I thought she was misremembering the name of the television weatherman.

"Yes, our thermometer," she retorted.

My grandmother was the most honest person I have ever known. She would not tell even white lies. It was the truth, the whole truth, and nothing but the truth for her. And she would never make promises either, for she said one could never know if one would always be in a position to keep them, that life was too unpredictable to be able to predict, to assume that what one offered without qualification to stand by one day could still be the case in time to come. She would say "Most likely, but I won't promise." I guess life for her was borne out to be uncertain, uncontrolled, and unsafe, dangereux. Never mind.

Having some recalcitrant, rebellious instincts, I would periodically try to test her limits. I would ask something by saying, "Would you promise that?" for instance, that we might go to the glamorous emporium of Penn Traffic the coming Saturday.

And she would invariably say, "I think it likely, but I cannot give my word. We don't know what the weather will be like. Or the car," things out of her control.

When I was five years old, I asked her the question that probably all children at some point ask a parent, "How old are you?"

Naturally, for my grandmother, this posed a moral dilemma. She did not want to lie, but she did not want to own up to being as ancient as fifty-eight years old.

So she said, "Over forty," as she later explained to me, though at the time all I heard was "Forty," which certainly sounded venerable enough to my young ears.

Some short time later, she was carpooling me and three of my little girl friends, the ice-skating clarinetists and another child, to school or somewhere. What was unusual about the families of these children was that they were all their families' youngest offspring, younger than much older siblings, which therefore, of course, rendered the mothers of these children much older than most mothers of five- and six-year-old children at that time.

My grandmother later recounted, though I have no recollection of this conversation, that she was aghast to hear, as we compared the ages of our respective maternal supervisors, that if she, Mrs. Raab, were indeed forty, then she was some years younger than these girls' mothers. In truth, Mrs. Raab, a generation beyond and already gray-haired, was most likely a decade or more their senior. All because of a variation on the truth told.

The supreme example of my testing her morality in this realm in what became, more accurately, a lesson for me, came one time around my birthday. Woolworth's alone, it seemed, carried a knights-and-ladies coloring book I coveted. And I made sure that my grandmother knew I wanted it. A few days before my birthday, I asked her if a recent shopping errand that she had run had included a stop at Woolworth's. There was no reason for me to inquire except out of mischief, and she had no other reason to go to Woolworth's except to buy the book for me.

She frowned. I could read her face. I was sure I knew what she was thinking. As with the little boy in William Wordsworth's poem, "Anecdote for Fathers," in which a parent's unremitting attempt to get the youngster to choose between the beach or the mountains as a preferred holiday spot causes the child finally just to lie to shut the parent up, my query forced her into an unwilling untruth. She did not want to deceive me, but she also did not want to ruin the surprise. I do not recall exactly what she said, and certainly, she chose her words carefully, but later, after my birthday and the presentation of the coloring book, she confessed to me that she had had to lie to maintain the secret of the present. I did not deserve that consideration. It is stunning now to think of someone's feeling the need to apologize to a child for such a seemingly understandable decision. But the near lie obviously felt like a transgression to her, and she was not going to live with that on her conscience or have me know that she could be a liar. It was a noble exemplum.

Properly, I was abashed and sorry, as I surely deserved to be. Nonetheless, I do not think I was honorable enough to confess to her that I had asked only to cause the moral dilemma. Now, much older, I see how rare that moral quandary is. I have not met many other people for whom lying is so painful, so difficult, and so wrong.

In her last two decades my grandmother was hospitalized several times for different afflictions, and the last two times in particular I visited her in the intensive-care unit of a local hospital. The first of these times, she was in renal failure, which her physician saw as astonishing, for, as he said to Aunt Marjie and me, "Did you know that she has three kidneys?" Much good they did to her, however, if they all went into failure at the same time. This occasioned some degree of speculation among her descendants, typified by the mental anguish my cousin David experienced. He said, "I felt as if, if I had three, I should surely volunteer to donate one of them to a stranger, but then I realized that what if some day my wife or daughter needed a kidney. It would be better for me to hang onto my spare for that eventuality." I think my grandmother would have appreciated that sense of altruism, and she liked David's wife.

Aunt Marjie and I went to see her in her hospital room in Intensive Care where we found her pulling weakly at a tube attached to her wrist, only vaguely alert. "Take this pocketbook from my arm, Laura, would you? The strap is weighing me down. It is too heavy for me right now," she said.

And then, looking around her more widely, not just at my aunt and me who were on either side of her bed but past us, she smiled and said, "Look at all the people who are here! There are Helen and Harry and Elizabeth and the others." Then, in a stage whisper, she added, "What are their names, Laura? I can never remember their names." And she smiled again as she welcomed this cloud of witnesses that she observed, who of course were not evident to us.

Later, the very last time I saw her alive, when I came alone to see her, again, in Intensive Care, she also described visitants from beyond the grave, calling out the names of long-dead cousins and aunts and uncles. It was a bit unnerving to observe because her voice sounded like herself and her eyes appeared to be open and sighted, yet what she saw was beyond my grasp. Perhaps she comprehended the other side of the Ouija board, perhaps she had pierced a veil between the here and now and something else, perhaps she had passed into Irish thin space? Then she gestured to me, because I had been standing back in awe of what she reported that she saw or imagined. "Come closer, Laura. Sit down," she commanded me.

I approached the chair by the bed and moved to sit down.

"Watch!" she exclaimed. "You just sat on Aunt Martha!"

She might have liked that connection to Wordsworth's poetry that I drew, a moment ago, for her love of English literature certainly extended to Wordsworth. I am sure that she was pleased that he was the subject of my dissertation. I have a copy of the red-bound, hardback collection of his poetry that she used at Vassar, along with the collections of Byron and Shelley from which she studied.

Earlier than the two incidents I have just mentioned, another Wordsworth connection arose. Once Penn Traffic closed, our options for upscale shopping became very limited, so that she and I would drive an hour and a half to a mall near Pittsburgh for the day. Our last time there, she fell and broke her hip. When she was hospitalized for surgery to repair the injury, she asked me to bring her the poem about "trailing clouds of glory." I was in college by this time and knew what poem she meant right away for I had just had a course in Romantic poetry, and already Wordsworth was one of my favorites.

I read the poem to her, and she said that it comforted her. It is a poem about loss and recovery and, for some, about the divine light that lingers at the edges of our lives, the embers that endure and give us hope amid life's tribulations, desolations, and griefs. Her philosophy of life matched these well expressed lines from this Great Ode of Wordsworth (also known as "Intimations of Immortality" and simply "Ode 'There was a time'"):

> Our birth is but a sleep and a forgetting:
> The Soul that rises with us, our life's Star,
> Hath had elsewhere its setting,

And cometh from afar:
Not in entire forgetfulness,
And not in utter nakedness,
But trailing clouds of glory do we come
From God, who is our home. . . (Lines 58–65)

I daresay that that was at the heart of my grandmother's faith, of what my grandmother believed, the means of consolation and strength, the source of her integrity and peace. For her, I am sure, Job's words rang true: 'For I know that my Redeemer lives, and that at the last he will stand upon the earth; and after my skin has been thus destroyed, then in my flesh I shall see God, whom I shall see on my side" (19: 25–27 [NRSV]), trailing clouds of glory.

Last, on one of the final occasions that I saw her in her room at the Allegheny Lutheran Home in Johnstown, where she dwelt the last eight years of her life, she received a phone call from a younger friend, the mother of my former dancing-lessons companion, who sought to tell her that the woman's mother-in-law, who had been a very good friend and bridge companion of my grandmother's, had died. My grandmother on that occasion, of course, seemed mindful of death, though I suspect that death was never far from her thoughts, while I, on the other hand, was full of thoughts of new life, for I had just driven from a job interview at a small Roman Catholic college not an hour away, also in Cambria County. I thought the interview had gone well and was feeling optimistic about my possibilities, while my grandmother must have been musing about that, too, for she said, anticipating my permanent relocation to some perhaps even more distant locale, "Are you still my little girl?"

I do not remember what I replied. I hope I mumbled some affirmation, but the question caught me off guard. I did not get an offer for that job; neither did I get an offer from another college in western Pennsylvania for which I interviewed around the same time, and I perforce took the offer for the only other position for which I interviewed, which became my thirty-year career, in Georgia, far, far away, as an English teacher, as my grandmother had been.

Time has passed, yet I know that, within the material and spiritual realities that my life has encountered, many waters cannot quench love, that my redeemer lives, that my grandmother is now reunited with my mother, and that both are watching over me beyond a mere Irish thin space, just a filament, a veil, a Ouija board, a prayer away, toward a place and a moment when the parallel converge.

v. Afterword: Mrs. Raab in Her Own Words

Sunday [autumn 1968]

Dear Marjie:

Thank you for the photos.

Do you have to furnish transportation for Fritz?

I have a suitcase of shells belonging to you.

This is a busy time for both Laura and me. She is banging out [likely typing on my mother's old manual typewriter] a letter to Connie while waiting for supper to cook. Why shouldn't I, too?

I broke down and took her to a Sunday matinee of "The Lion in Winter." It must have been o.k., as three nuns sat in our row! However, I would not recommend it for any of your children, altho' the M-rated pictures are harmless for Laura. From what I hear, some of her associates use strong (?) language and tell stories she says she can't understand! I don't ask her to repeat them. This movie has some ugly words. But Laura said, "If royalty lived like pigs, they must have talked like pigs also." I feel it is a powerful picture, really deserving the word "tremendous." It has a lot of depth both in philosophy and in acting. I hope I can see it again!

Tonight Laura is going to resume membership in EYC [Episcopal Young Churchmen]. When I introduced her to the new priest, he said, "'Dabundo.' That must be Irish." He has a delightful wit. His pretty wife [*] was there in the shortest dress in the Parish—and that is very, very short! [The wife of a high-school friend of my aunt Marjie's] said, "I see where I should have to shorten my dresses." As she is in the choir, I suggested that all members do so. I'll bet that would bring out the men, the authorities are always angling for! [*side note to provide maiden name and hometown of the rector's wife, also the hometown of my aunt's husband]

Yesterday Laura went to a home [high-school football] game, after which twenty-one girls went to S.'s for dinner. This is the fourth time Mrs. S. has fed S's friends. She is a super cook. In the P.M. the girls held a séance in which [the daughter of a woman with whom my aunt had gone to summer camp] was the medium. She has dramatic skill, but her speaking for Vachel Lindsay left much to be desired. Laura caught several errors!

Laura's memory amazes me, but is a great help to me also. She loves history, and we both feel [your son] is missing a good thing. I suppose he will get it later.

On Friday I suddenly became very ill. I had a severe pain in my back for three days and the 24 Hour Bug—or something—really knocked me out. I had had a shot on Wed., and I had expected to be well all winter as I was last year. However, something went wrong.

Eager to hear "in-depth" news of all of you. Almost time for sizes and suggestions for Christmas!

Love to all, Mother

2

Celtic Travels

i. Pilgrim, Tread Softly, for This Is Hallowed Ground

With apologies to Martin Buber

Twelve hundred years before
A pride of dark-enshrouded forms
Heavily cowled and virtuously cloistered,
Wove through the gorse and nettles
Down the centuries past
To the well or spring or creek
That bubbled up.

The billowing pillows cross patterns
In a gray and restless sky
Mimicking the wooly sheep that range the fields
Beneath.

I looked into the eye of a ewe
Or ram,
And, registering together, I and ewe,
It became I and thou for a moment.

She came sweetly toward me,
Agnes of God.

And so, pilgrim, later,
Weave you softly too
Holy ground lies beneath us,
Holy Erin
I and thou.

ii. Welsh Waters

a.

Hemmed in by hedges, grown tall and taller,
Creeping more closely across the lanes,
They lightly caress the coach on either side,
Provide a labyrinth of corridors
That leads to the pilgrims' hoped-for thin space.

b.

Draping the fell like an old woman's shawl,
The fog sinks down through the verdant valleys,
Dampening and muting the colors
Emeralds and ochers and umbers.
It forms a coverlet of squares and fringes
Made of puffy hedgerows, hardly hedgerows.
As the fog shifts and lifts,
A horizon emerges.
Intermittently sharp corners of gray and brown edifices appear to
poke through.
The fog collapses upon the sheer fineness,
A silvery and almost white opacity
Of the lake,
Still and hardly rippled.
On the near bank, sedge and weeds

Evoke Mosaic mysteries of birth and life,
Everlasting and unchanging,
Even as it varies from moment to moment.

c.

The church tower is blunt and Norman,
Foursquarely cutting through the landscape
Heavensward and heavensfield.
Meadow and marsh and lake
Lift up mine eyes unto the hills
From whence cometh my help.

d.

Now the rain dissolves hill and lake and grass
Into the wet and watery silvery whiteness.
Water and lake and holy springs
Merging sky and land, spirit and flesh, heaven and earth, and life
and death,
Into a pilgrims' thin space.
You and me and all of us
Together now and for all time
World without end.

iii. Thin Space

Jesus said, "Foxes have holes, and birds of the air have nests,
but the Son of Man has nowhere to lay his head."

LUKE 9:58 (NRSV)

At last, the plane, which would take me home to Atlanta from the
North Jersey airport, was set to take off. It was after midnight, now

turned Friday at the end of June; the flight was full; I was sitting in the middle seat of the bulkhead row, but I did not care. It was a plane heading to Atlanta; I was onboard and going home.

I had just participated in a two-week pilgrimage of eighteen erstwhile strangers to Ireland. Spiritual matters attract me, though I find it difficult to put into words what they might mean, what they are. However, in Ireland, our group did not have to talk about these matters. We felt them, and we came together as we stood in the cool currents of St. Patrick's Cathedral in Dublin; outdoors, we walked on the gravel paths of St. Columba's ancient church at Drumcliffe; we traversed the grounds of a ruined medieval monastery under the tall shadows of a carved high cross and crumbling round tower. It was an easy trick of the imagination to catch the sudden swirl of a cassock around the corner of a ruined choir, to hear a chant's fading echo amid the songs of birds. We walked the paths of the past and were haunted by its spirits. The Irish of every generation seem to have sought burial on these hallowed grounds; consequently we were surrounded by Celtic crosses from long ago, as well as from practically just last week. The older ones were lichen-covered, mossy, but everything was receding into time past and preserving time present at once and for all time. Everything had a place and had a stillness.

Farther out-of-doors into the fields of sheep and cattle and even more deeply into the past, we clambered over styles between dry-stone walls to reach ancient stone circles, smaller than Stonehenge but just as myth-laden, and reconstructed labyrinths, circling in the ground, bringing us away from the everyday world to a silent center and then arcing back out, refreshed, renewed. In all of these places, I could sense the connections, the consolations, and profound peace across time and space. My fellow pilgrims had assembled from all over our country, teachers, accountants, librarians, consultants, resulting in an informal fellowship of support and affection.

All of these recollections and sensations jumbled in my mind as the plane was taking off. I was eager to get home to try to sort it all out, to separate the quick from the dead and to achieve some meanings to take forward in my daily life.

Gracefully, the plane eased from the gate.

It had been a long Thursday for me. It had begun in Dublin twenty hours before when I arose in the early hours for transport to the airport where I learned that rainstorms in the area of New York were delaying the plane's arrival from America. My plane made a loop between North Jersey and Dublin every day, so that the plane that would take me stateside needed first to come from North Jersey to fetch the other passengers and me.

The apologetic Monumental airlines clerk gave me a ten-Euro voucher toward breakfast. The computer evidently balked, and she had some slight delay processing my two checked bags. She shrugged, "I'll just check these by hand. That'll be fine."

Two hours later, having a final Irish breakfast with blood pudding and then trying fitfully to read while waiting at the gate, I watched my fellow travelers accumulate with their excessive carry-on bags. It became apparent that our delayed eight-hour flight would arrive after the time of departure of my connecting flight home.

Dejected, I returned to the apologetic clerk at the check-in counter, passing by the security guards whom I would then have to re-pass and again display my plastic bags and my shoes, while standing in my stocking feet. This time, she promised me a seat on the next flight to Atlanta from North Jersey after the one I was supposed to be on. "Don't worry," she said reassuringly. "You will have a seat on the next flight; just confirm it when you get to North Jersey." And she handed me a seven-Euro voucher for lunch this time.

Another two hours later, the plane arrived from America, was cleaned of the detritus of the arriving tourists, and filled up with us. I had the aisle seat at the back of the plane in the penultimate row, next to a young couple who had the window and middle seats. I realized into the flight that they were the parents of three little red-headed girls who sat together across the aisle from me on the other side of the plane. It was curious to me that the family was divided in two by me, that it surrounded me. As nearly as I could determine, the girls were triplets of indeterminate but some undisciplined age, in whom, as I came to learn, their mother had completely lost interest. She spent her time gazing out the window, drinking up all the wine with which her husband devotedly plied her, while he fortified himself with coffee and tried, across my lap, to instill decorum in his daughters. His efforts were to no avail. Any time we had to be buckled in for takeoff, landing, or turbulence, the squirming girls squirted out of their seat belts, screaming at one another, pinching and crawling over one another. On those occasions their parents seemingly never heard them. Was I, the middleman now in the family, supposed to intervene? What about the drunken mother? Any time the children needed a parent's attention, a little girl hollered, "Dad!"

After a couple hours, the father announced to me, "Now, we'll trade seats for a while."

"Oh, no!" I stared at him in alarm. "I am very claustrophobic. I deliberately reserved an aisle seat for this trip."

Nonplused, he waited until I fell asleep, then unceremoniously and vengefully awakened me so he could get out to the aisle. By the end of the flight, we had achieved an apparent but unstated ceasefire.

Long- or short-term peace was not to be my fate, for the North Jersey airport was a disaster area. Sheer mayhem reigned. Following instructions, the newly arrived marched down the long corridors to Immigration and Passport Control, down escalators, in lockstep, loaded with gear, loaded for bear, headed for the line that would then split to the enclosed counters, like pedestrian tollbooths on some immigration highway, where dour bureaucrats skimmed our passports, scrutinized our visages. They matched the slumberous, travel-weary faces with the manic, wanted-poster-like images preserved for a decade on our official entry cards. Astonishingly, my gatekeeper looked up at me, nearly smiled, and said, "Welcome home." I was cheered and ready for International Baggage Claim.

Alas, I had another stop to make beforehand. I had to confirm my reservation for my connecting flight. At the maw of International Baggage Claim, high above his empire on a tall stool sat the air-traffic controller of this realm, in front of an all-knowing computer screen. People pushed and shoved to get in a line before/beside/behind him? It was not clear from his position where we were supposed to queue up.

I shoved my well-worn ticket at him.

"You've missed your connection, you have."

"I know that. But in Dublin the Monumental agent said. . ."

"Yeah." He interrupted me. "You are on Flight 85, the seven o'clock flight to Atlanta. It is now nine o'clock here. But that flight is delayed until 10:30. How many bags do you have? According to the screen, you have none." He glared at me accusingly, it seemed, daring me to have entrusted my baggage to the airline.

I told him. And I wondered if the helpful Dublin agent had misreported the record of my luggage.

"Claim your bags. Go through those doors at the far end. Get to your flight. Next."

It took the eternity it always seems that it does for the bags from our flight to arrive, but I had until after ten o'clock, so I would could relax. We all watched the volcano high near the ceiling disgorge, from the depths of the airport, in random spurts, suitcases of all sizes and dimensions though nearly all black in color, golf-club bags, valises, baby strollers, garment bags, an eruption of personal possessions shot up violently, explosively, threateningly. And then the bags cascaded down the moving ramp, determined to pile up and spill or else block the succeeding descent of all other objects of profound personal prejudice. Everyone stationed around me threw themselves at the carousel to wrench their own bags from the centripetal force of the relentless orbit before, at last, my bags, dazed and scuffed, it seemed, hurtled from oblivion into my eager purchase.

I tried to organize my biggest bag upright on its wheels and attach my smaller bag and my carry-on onto its extended handle somehow, and, swinging my handbag over my shoulder, I aimed my edifice of luggage at the double doors to which the guardian of this empire had directed me.

However, passage through those doors caused my house-of-cards of organized luggage to collapse, disintegrating on the floor into its separate pieces. Despairing, I saw lines upon lines upon lines of heavy laden humanity, all trying gamely to pull, push, and steer similarly ungainly vehicles of luggage forward. I rebuilt my tower of luggage.

Thin young men in blue uniforms barked at us. "This way! This way! Don't stand in the way! Keep moving!"

I obeyed and approached the agent in charge of another moving carousel, this one for connecting flights. I disassembled my luggage.

"Let me see your ticket," he said. "You need to go through there to rebook."

"I am rebooked."

"You need to go over there to the International Counter," he gestured vaguely over his shoulder, "You need to get your ticket there."

Dutifully, I reassembled my luggage tower yet again and towed it along the river of humanity that surged around me. Brilliantly clad children, adults in sweat-drenched sportswear, teenagers falling out of minimal clothing, burka-clad Muslim women, sari-draped Indian women, I in my yellow rain slicker that would not fit in any of my luggage, we all were borne along an irresistible tide toward a wide, empty counter. No one was there. But around it swirled a vast serpentine current of humanity, several people across, dozens, hundreds, all towing or stationed by their luggage. Was it a line?

"Where is the end of this line?"

"You can't stand here! Go to the end of the line! Back there! Back there! We've been in line for three hours! You can't get ahead of us! Back there! Back there!" A cacophony of voices shouted at me and all of the rest of us trying to join the line.

I wandered in circles and finally stationed myself at the foot of an escalator. Other people rapidly eddied behind me so I guessed it was a line. We never moved. Children squalled. Men and women pushed and shoved. My feet were trod upon. My luggage tower swayed and toppled. I was perspiring.

"You can't stand here! Go to the end of the line! Back there! Back there! We've been in line for three hours! You can't get ahead of us! Back there! Back there!" The newcomers to the line picked up the chants of the veterans.

Nine thirty PM.

Nine forty-five. I am going to miss my flight.

Behind me, a man wearing an orange tie was calling his airline. But of course he was on hold. Were not we all? He told me he was trying to get home to Houston. He had been in China. Around us sailed a family in dashikis, several children and parents, looking tired and hot.

"I have a flight," I said. "But I can't get to it; I couldn't check my bags."

"Here," the man with the orange tie said, his face crinkling in kindness. "You can use my phone when I get off. If I ever get off."

The African father looked at me sternly, "Go back there and make them take your bags. Get to your gate."

"Yes, yes," his wife added. Her dark eyes were warm and soft. "We'll save your space in line for you if you have to come back."

The two men concurred and practically pushed me out of the line. Did they want my spot? I realized with a start that they were looking out for me, making a personal connection in this otherwise inhumane spot of impossible and lost connections.

"Thank you." I smiled at my benefactors, who had appeared like rare lights in this gray and hostile landscape.

"Go!"

I heaved my luggage forward, trying to keep it upright. Every few steps it fell over. I returned to the domain of blue uniforms and found a young woman who seemed to be in charge.

As concisely as I could, I explained, "I have a ticket for a flight that hasn't left yet, but I'm afraid I am going to miss it."

"Here, over here." She led me to a counter where a tall-hatted woman, whose rambunctious children crawled over her as if she were a tree, was berating an agent in front of a computer monitor. My agent elbowed in, took charge, and began to type.

"Yes, here you are. Let me see your ticket. Hmmm. This is strange." She showed it to the besieged agent, who agreed, who clearly wanted to agree with everyone and everything. "No luggage checked, but your bags have tags." The Dublin agent strikes again.

Ten o'clock.

"Here, I'll check your bags again." Two minutes. "Take your bags over to the counter and then go to Terminal C and the gate for Flight 85."

"How do I get there?"

"Just follow the signs."

Terminal C, where are you? Where am I? Lost and alone in a vast airport of multiple terminals, crowded with angry people, I towed my luggage tower toward the carousel.

"No, no, here, here." The blue-suited agents were imperious. I surrendered my bags where they specified and then turned to find the signs.

Back through the serpentine swirl, up the escalator.

Ten fifteen.

Signs indicated that I had to take a train to distant terminals, like C. Up another escalator to a platform. Which side? Where was I going? My stomach was tied in knots. It was a good thing that I had not had anything to eat in a while. I waited on the platform with a few other people.

A train that reminded me of a small European one divided into compartments within the cars clickety-clacked to a stop. According to the signs, it would take me to Terminal C. With everyone else just standing behind me, I pried a door open, and half a dozen of us tumbled in. No one seemed very happy to be sharing this space. And not all of us could sit. I sat. I had earned a seat by my mechanics with the door.

We rode through Terminals A and B and rumbled to C. My stop. I dashed out, dragging my handbag and carry-on.

Down an escalator I sprinted to Security. Again. The third time today. If it was still today.

Fortunately, there was no line.

"Do I need to take off my shoes?" I asked, as I assembled my possessions, shed my slicker, and placed everything on the plastic tubs on which it would ride through the X-ray machine.

"Sure." The TSA agent concurred. I had the feeling that if I had not asked, I could have left them on.

I strode through the open booth of the check.

Where do I go from here? I asked, but no one answered.

Down a long hall I raced, till it came to a corner and seemed to end. Where to now? I turned around and hurried back toward Security. I could see that the agents turned to me and looked with mild interest but made no attempt to assist me out of my perplexity. A well-dressed family of four or five appeared from behind where I had been.

"Where are the gates?"

They ignored me. The wife glared at me. No community feeling here. Together, we hurried around the corner in the hall. It opened up into the terminal. We darted by gates where crowds of people waited for planes, lined up to get on, and other gates, now emptied of humanity but filled with the flotsam and jetsam of departed travelers, silent and deserted. The minutes flashed on.

10:25.At last, at the very end of the hall, in an ambit of four gates, I saw the sign for the gate for Monumental 85 to Atlanta and stumbled onto the carpet of the waiting area. People were still sitting, not yet lined up to board. A woman was reaching into a pet carrier to poke at an animal inside. Children were scuttling around, crashing into people and luggage. Adults were desultorily turning the pages of newspapers and magazines. Several uniformed airline workers loitered at the front of the counter. They were arguing about which of them would find seats on an overbooked flight to their destinations for the extended Memorial Day holiday, which is what had filled up all the planes today, contributing massively to the crowding when flights were delayed or canceled.

Passengers talked to the agent at the counter. We waited.

The sign behind the counter never changed from announcing, "Atlanta. Flight 85. Ten thirty."

The minutes ticked on. Perspiration dripped from me, so I took off my slicker.

Finally, at eleven fifteen, an agent strolled to the desk and opened boarding. The Brahmins of the American system of airline travel—businessmen, frequent flyers, first-class passengers—boarded while many others tried to sneak on, defiantly or surreptitiously or ostentatiously or cavalierly, trying to slide by an agent they hoped was benighted and unsuspecting. This agent was having none of that and kept sending people back, so a line to board the plane formed amid throngs of people holding their breath, waiting to burst onto the plane.

Eventually, I was in my seat, belt cinched. Eventually, the plane glided toward the runway. Outside it was dark, and it seemed to be dry, though the tarmac glistened from light reflecting in puddles left from the earlier rains. The night looked still. The lights were almost star-like. I was at peace. The men on either side of me seemed to fall asleep almost immediately.

We had not yet begun to taxi when our peace was interrupted. "This is your captain speaking. There is a problem. We are going back to the terminal." Pause. "The FAA has regulations for how long a crew can be on duty. This crew has now exceeded that limit by six minutes. At the gate, you'll be told what to do."

Loud murmurings burst into shrill voices: "What!" "How dare they?" "They can't do this to us!" "Who do they think they are?" The rage was hot, palpable. A passenger assailed a steward who had the misfortune to walk past the row behind me: "It's all your fault. If you all hadn't wasted time trying to figure out which of you would get to go on this flight, we wouldn't have lost six minutes. We would be in the air now." The steward shrugged and kept on moving, but his ears turned red.

All evening long I had heard snatches of irate conversations, from the terminal to the plane. Grumbling about delayed planes, delayed bags, canceled flights, long lines, and no attention. Attention must be paid. And now this. I did not need to say anything at all as we departed from the plane. Everyone else spoke my thoughts: What now? Where to go? Would there be an alternative crew? Would there be an alternative flight? When? I was engulfed, carried along, by an infuriated mob of mostly businessmen. In the terminal right ahead of me, a man in a pin-striped suit and loosened tie hurled his briefcase down on the floor. It burst opened, spilling out jockey shorts. Hastily he stuffed them back in and stomped off to join the other enraged passengers who stormed the lone attendant manning the barricades against us.

"Is Monumental supplying another crew?" Someone demanded of her.

"I don't know."

"Is there another flight?"

"Not tonight, no."

"Is Monumental canceling this flight?"

"I don't know."

"What are we supposed to do?'

"I don't know."

Over and over again. As if she were an automaton, dispatched to stand guard, the airline agent dispensed her virtually pre-recorded message. Monumental had put her there with no resources to deal with what she faced. After about fifteen minutes, the phone at the counter rang. She answered it, listened, and then picked up the microphone. "Flight 85 to Atlanta is canceled. Passengers should go to Domestic Baggage Claim to retrieve their bags." She put down the mic.

Groans and curses, anger and resentment from the displaced passengers met her announcement.

I found a payphone and tried to call Monumental. An automated answering system put me on hold. Around me people on cell phones were clearly also on hold. A voice on my call, after interminable lilting dance music, intoned: "Your wait will be twenty minutes." I hung up and decided to make my way to Domestic Baggage Claim.

As I trudged there, I passed three policemen abreast hurrying toward the gate where I had been. "There is a lot of anger over there," one of them bent his head to tell his shoulder.

Others from my flight were ahead of me and already at Domestic Baggage Claim, revolving around a stationary carousel and themselves rolling into the office beside it.

"No," declared the attendant. "You cannot get your bags. This is not a secure area. Monumental will not release your bags this evening. They will be on the first flight later this morning, Friday morning, to Atlanta."

"But none of us will be on it."

"I don't know anything about that, but I cannot let you have your bags now."

"Do you know that there are no available hotel rooms around the airport?" one man proclaimed.

Others nodded, and another man added, "It is a holiday weekend. All the flights were already filled up before this, and all the hotel rooms gone before we were stranded."

A small woman in a flowered dress wailed, "Monumental put me on a flight Sunday morning. I'll be back home before I leave here."

"What do you mean?" I asked.

"I was trying to get to Atlanta for a funeral on Saturday. But my flight to Atlanta now is scheduled for Sunday, while my return flight from Atlanta is Saturday night."

"Can you believe that?"

"That is true for me, too," said another woman.

Beyond the carousels there were rows of fixed plastiform seats. A few people slouched in them, surrounded by their piles of carry-on bags. I did not know what to do. It was the middle of the night. I was alone in an unfamiliar airport in an unfamiliar city, the veritable stranger in a strange land. I was back in America, in my own country, and yet I felt farther distant from anything known than I had ever felt any time I was in Ireland. Here I was marooned in a terminal. I felt terminal. When and how would I ever get home?

Seeing my evident distress, a middle-aged man seated next to another man, who was himself slumped over with his eyes closed and his mouth open, asked me, "Where are you trying to go?"

I told him.

"Oh. We're going to Jacksonville. We've been upstate. I guess we're getting there. Just sit down here. Relax. It will be all right." He smiled at me.

I sat. A handsome young man in a navy suit who had been on my aborted flight—I had noticed him back at the gate—sat beside me. A young blonde woman paced nearby.

He told me that he and his bride were planning a getaway for the weekend. He looked at his watch. "I guess we could go back into the city. I have an apartment there. I don't have to stay here all night." The woman did not seem to like his talking to me. But I was grateful that both of these men had spoken to me, had extended a moment of connection.

I decided to walk around, my one piece of baggage and my handbag, dangling from each shoulder. What else could I do? I did not want to sit there forever. If only I could get to Pyramid Airlines, I decided. Pyramid would get me to Atlanta, would get me home. But none of the arrival and departure signs listed Pyramid flights.

At that time, I did not have a cellphone. Therefore, I wandered several hundred yards to a payphone and called Pyramid.

"Pyramid does not fly out of North Jersey. But if you go to JFK, we can put you on standby. It is a holiday weekend, though, and everything is full."

"Thanks. I am going to review my options."

What options? I was stuck in New Jersey in the middle of the night and had no idea when I might get home. Home seemed infinitely distant. I decided I needed to call Monumental just to verify a seat on a flight for which I had already paid, but I did not expect to have any better luck than any of my almost fellow travelers had had.

Predictably, the agent cheerily put me on the Sunday morning flight of which I had already heard. "You'll leave for Atlanta at 8 AM," she assured me gaily. "Do you want to make your seat assignment now?"

"Yeah." Why not?

I wandered up a short escalator to the next level. This was Ticketing. But it was deserted. Wherever I roamed in the airport, there were people asleep. Some people slept sitting up or slouched over. One resourceful person lay with his back on the floor, his head on clothing folded under it, his arms hemmed in by luggage, and his legs up and over the chair. Two people lay on the floor facing each other, with their luggage at their heads and on the chairs over them, guarding them. Hardly anyone was awake. No one else seemed to be wandering around like me.

I saw on a screen that Amalgamated Airlines had a six AM flight to Atlanta. I would get on that, I decided. I would get in line before anyone else, and I would get on that plane.

Two AM.

I espied a V-shaped arrangement of seats with just two people, both dozing, facing each other across the V. I sat down about three seats from the woman. She had a bag that said "Womanspirit." That sounded safe to me.

And I dozed. And slept. And dreamed. And remembered.

I dreamed about red-headed triplet girls like witches dancing and singing and disks of blood pudding and angry passengers and volcanoes of luggage and blue-uniformed agents and winding, endless lines up and down and around and on escalators and trains and planes. Always planes. Countless planes. People, people everywhere, yelling, screaming, dragging mounds of luggage, and then hurling the suitcases at one another, at airport employees, and at me, while I dodged and darted. It was a surreal vision out of DeQuincey's *Confessions of an English Opium Eater*.

Then I awoke a bit. Suddenly I remembered what had happened two now distant weeks ago when I first was in the North Jersey airport, on the first leg of my trip so long ago. My flight from Atlanta had been delayed—an omen—and I wound up on another flight. But I arrived in North Jersey and made my way to the gate of the Dublin flight with two hours till departure. So I decided to eat, just to pass the time.

I saw a familiar pizza outlet, which seemed reassuring for I used to frequent one in Newark, Delaware—a serendipity of new arks, vehicles of security—years ago when I lived there, so there I went, taking my place in line behind a host of indecisive diners. When it was my turn, finally, I loaded up on spaghetti and maneuvered my tray, my pocketbook, my carry-on, and myself to the last remaining table, one for four.

Before I had even seated myself, while I was still arranging my items, a man's voice interrupted me, "Do you mind if I sit at this table?" He appeared neat, clean, middle-aged, and intelligent.

"Sure," I shrugged, meaning the opposite. Or not. I am not one to talk much to strangers.

We sat cattycornered from each other.

I ate.

He had several dishes on his tray. "You look like a wise woman," he said.

I stared at him.

"You are, you know. You know you are. A wise woman. Out of the Wiccan understanding. Do you know those ideas?"

I nodded for I did not know what to say.

"Spiritual, in touch with what is around us, profoundly, deeply around us. Not the surface, but the enduring."

I smiled at him. "I am interested in those things."

"Yes," he said. "I can tell."

"In fact," I said, "I am going to Ireland now, which is a kind of spiritual home for me."

"Are you Irish? Black Irish? My mother is. Was. She died a few years ago." He looked off into the distance, with grief in his eyes.

"Distantly Irish, I am. More Italian than Irish. Where are you going?"

He told me he was going to Brazil and that he and his wife traveled frequently to interesting places, Greece, Turkey, elsewhere in South America. He was a business consultant, I gathered. We talked a bit about those deeper things, those lasting and enduring connections beneath the shallow and superficial workaday world of everyday living, where spirits console and find peace. We discussed Wiccan lore, Christian traditions, Eastern archetypes, touching variegated beliefs that acknowledge another world, a reality of shadows and spirits, of myths and truths. He had studied in California—of course—at Esalen and other places, but he was working out his own kind of understanding, his own kinds of connections, borrowed from the many traditions of the East and the West. And then he chanted a Wiccan hymn for me, softly, gently, and beautifully. It spoke of time and tides, of wind and waves, of peace and gentleness, of wisdom and acceptance, of sun and moon and sky and stars and worlds away from here. It was soothing and pleasant and for a few moments took me away from the bustle of the airport.

I was captivated. All of these things that he said, that we discussed, were a part and parcel of what was drawing me to Ireland, to the land of saints and scholars. "I would like to learn more about what you have described. Could you recommend something for me to read?"

He looked a little startled but also pleased. "Let me think. You might read Starhawk. D. T. Suzuki. Stephen Mitchell." He paused. "You have a birthday coming up soon."

I was dumfounded. Had he seen my passport? My driver's license, when I was might have fumbled to pay for my food? Or somehow when I checked in? But no one had been standing near me on any of those occasions. "My birthday is in August."

"You are a wise woman, as I said, and I am a wise man. And you are blessed. You know the Irish traveler's blessing? Good. My name is Brian, which is Gaelic, so I can say this to you. Do you mind if I say it for you?

> May the road rise up to meet you.
> May the wind be always at your back.
> May the sun shine warm upon your face;
> the rains fall soft upon your fields and until we meet again,
> may God hold you in the palm of His hand.

"Thank you very much," I said. "This is all very extraordinary to me. Do you know the concept of thin spaces in Celtic spirituality?"

He shook his head.

"It is that there are spaces, thin places, like Jacob's ladder, places where the spiritual world and the temporal world, the dream world and the real world, the world of eternity and the world of time, meet and dissolve together, the place where ghosts or angels or visitors from another plane stand beside mortals, visible, for a moment of transcendence." I paused. I was a bit embarrassed.

Brian smiled. "I think that this moment is a thin space. I shall remember you and this time." He asked me my name, and then we both left for our flights and our travels commenced.

Two weeks later, my bewitched, bedeviled return to the North Jersey airport on a holiday weekend and my fruitless attempts to return home.

Awakened now from my slumber in the North Jersey airport, after the unfortunate and failed endeavors on Friday evening to get home, I looked at my watch. 3:45 AM. Well, whatever came of all of this dark night and whenever I got home, I had had a good trip, certainly. I had wandered among such holy and haunted sites as the medieval monastic ruins of Glendalough; climbed the hill of Knocknarea, cairn of Queen Maeve, the fairy queen; seen from afar the craggy holy isle of Skellig Michael; visited the basilica at Knock where the Virgin Mary had herself visited; marveled at a fairy mount of trees and mosses in a field outside Bundoran; and descended into the dark depths of the prehistoric mounds at Knowth with their own abiding secrets. All of these places moved me profoundly as I stood where for centuries pagans and Christians had sought and found solace and connection. These were places of pilgrimage, and I too was a traveler, a pilgrim, a seeker. But was I a wise woman? I did not imagine that the family of triplets whom I would not interact with on my flight from Dublin would think so.

I drifted off to sleep again and returned to the realm of dreams where I was visited with images of long-robed monks in green fields and witchy women in oak forests and druids in misty marshes against a landscape of round towers, high crosses, passage tombs, carven saints, and sheela-na-gigs.

For the last time, I woke again. Alone. My two fellow sleepers had silently vanished some time in the night. It was now 4:15. I had slumbered near the Amalgamated ticket counter; therefore, I gathered my possessions and staggered toward a line that was already taking shape.

Another hour of my life spent waiting in an airline terminal. Here, I struck up a conversation with a woman from Sacramento and men from Montana and Chicago. They had all been stranded by canceled Amalgamated flights the day before, which did not bode well, I inferred, for the likelihood of my getting on the Atlanta flight I desired. The woman told me how to get into New York and out again to Kennedy if I chose the Pyramid option since I did not yet have an Amalgamated booking. The woman advised me to speak to a roving Amalgamated agent. She motioned the agent over to me.

"I want to get home to Atlanta," I pleaded.

"We are all full up; the holiday weekend and then the weather have just messed everyone's schedule up," she said. "Go to Spartan-Fly. It has lots of flights to Atlanta."

The woman from Sacramento wished me Godspeed. And I wished her well, too. Our conversation had made my wait more bearable.

Off I trundled to SpartanFly where a flight to Atlanta was posted for seven AM. I waited in line for about twenty minutes. An obliging agent sold me a standby seat for three hundred dollars. Credit cards are very helpful. At the gate I stood in line, developing the swift camaraderie of travel in which I was now expert. Other standby flyers told me that standby on SpartanFly was their favored way of travel. One woman was going to visit her dying father. "I forgot, though, that it was Memorial Day weekend," she grimaced.

Espying another phone stand, I called a friend back home. She talked to her partner who offered to drive the more than 1400 miles to North Jersey and back to bring me home. Astounding generosity! I demurred to see if the airlines could do the trick in less time. My fortunes were commencing to change.

None of us secured seats on that flight, but the agent, who was the same man who had sold me my ticket, said to me, "Come back for the noon flight. I think I can help you then." I was touched by his gesture. His eyes looked sincere.

Sitting at the gate, I talked to a kindly social worker from New Jersey, who was flying with her husband to the funeral of their foster son in North Georgia. It seemed to me that death was a common reason for much travel. She offered to buy me something to eat and then to share her bun with me, but I was past hunger, thirst, or exhaustion, though I probably epitomized all of those. It felt like days since I had eaten or slept in a bed. It was very kind of her, I thought, surely in the midst of her grieving, to be concerned for me.

"Stand at the desk," she advised me. "Oblige them to take you."

I did.

And they did. And they got my standby companions on the flight, too. And the plane's crew could not have been more considerate of the needs of this band of weary travelers. I felt as if I were flying with angels. There had been angels all along in my dark night of the soul, in my experience of thin spaces in the North Jersey airport when I had no place to lay my head—the apologetic clerk in Dublin, the man from Houston and the African-clad family, the female agent who found my flight, the man from Jacksonville, the sleeping woman with the Womanspirit bag, the woman from Sacramento, the roving Amalgamated agent, the SpartanFly agent, my friend's partner, the kindly social worker, my fellow standbys, and Brian the wise man, at the beginning. The stewards on this flight supplied me with something to drink and something to eat and inquired if I were comfortable. Everywhere, the parallel generosity of others had benefited me, with no thought of their own recompense. That is one way in which the parallels converge. But my trek was not yet over.

When I arrived, at last, in Atlanta, and stumbled to the Monumental baggage claim office, the agent there said, "Oh, yes, all the bags from Flight 85 are there. Right there."

"Mine aren't there."

"Well, wait for the bags from the flight you just took, then," he snapped.

"I flew SpartanFly."

He stared at me. I looked again through the sea of bags. And found my two, which had been hand checked in Dublin, then re-checked in North Jersey.

Exiting the airport, I emerged into the sun to get my ride home.

3

Infirmities

i. Let This Mortal Flesh Be Silent

The pain comes like a dagger piercing my eye and penetrating to
my scalp.
I am standing at my sink, and I drop everything to race through
the house to get away
        from the pain,
Ending upstairs with my face buried in my pillow.
It passes as quickly as it came.
Twenty-six hours later it returns.
Three times.
Three days.
Then medicine dampens it, lessens it.
But there are other symptoms.

I thought that visions of mortality meant death,
To grieve the loss of loved ones was to feel the presence of one's
own end time.
That that was how one gathered intimations of mortality.
But I was wrong.

Shingled, scabbed, scarred, stricken,
"That this too solid, sullied flesh would melt,"
He knew it, felt it.

Stabbed, scratched.
There is a mortality of feeling, of pain, of incapacity and limitations.
The body pulls against one's efforts to glide effortlessly through this world
As youth, the fit, the infatuated do.

One feels each moment of pain as darkness.
The body cries out,
It grabs and pulls and punches and yells.
I want to learn its language
Of presence, of immediacy
So I can shut it up.

ii. My Eventful Year: A Pilgrimage of Healing

a. Losing My Life

A close friend remarked to me last summer, "When all this is over with, you will have lost two and maybe three months of your life." Maybe so, maybe not. Let's consider. What was my life up to this watershed year? According to the Enneagram of personality types, I am a nearly perfect Five—introspective, scholarly, abstracted, reserved, and content to live my life as a disembodied head with minimal physical presence in the world. I had a love/hate relationship with my body. Most of the time, I wished it would just vanish, but then where would I be, how could I be in the everyday work-a-day world? Accordingly, I labored on, most of the time fat, though periodically but infrequently and only after mammoth dieting and exercising, thin-ish, but ever rebounding to my true heavy bodily state, which I mostly ignored. I had had a career that enabled me to get away with this and to live intellectually because I was an English professor and had rather to be mentally alive than to be physically active.

At the beginning of May 2014, I officially retired, though I continued to teach part-time. Thus, I lived in my mind and also in my Episcopal church, where I was a lay reader and Eucharistic minister on Sundays and Wednesdays and also attended Morning Prayer every week day. (Morning Prayer is a formal liturgy, a sequence of scriptural readings and prayers of the Episcopal Church, which can be led by a lay person.) Additionally, at home, I followed and supplemented a daily devotional, highly structured prayer and Bible reading routine, based in part on prayers of the Anamchara Fellowship, a dispersed monastic community of men and women of the Episcopal Church of which I am a lay Companion. Moreover, I had completed training at the Haden Institute at Kanuga, NC, and was a spiritual director for several women. I had good friends with whom I socialized and community literary groups that I enjoyed. My life was orderly, predictable, and satisfactory.

For eighteen or so months up to May 2016, I had diligently exercised at twice weekly sessions at my employer's fitness center, following two months of physical therapy for osteoarthritis of the knees, as well as for general fitness and strength training. I worked each time under the direction of a supervised student. I had had several different guides, many of whom tried assiduously to devise varying routines for each 45-minute session. Then, in what became the last time, we tried a new procedure in which I held a weighted disk in front of my chest and swung it side to side for a number of repetitions. I accomplished that, probably at my usual mediocre level, along with all the other exercises. All was well until that very evening when lower-back pain led me to surmise that I must have pulled a muscle.

The next morning the pain had intensified so much that movement was difficult. I texted a friend who also attended Morning Prayer to let her know I would not be coming to the 8 AM service. Instead of going to church, however, she stopped at my house to see how I was. She encouraged me to call my internist and then went to the drugstore for the muscle relaxant he prescribed. The medicine knocked me out all afternoon, evening, and night, but the next morning, it took me fifteen minutes to get out of bed and to the bathroom. The pain was excruciating. I struggled down the stairs and plopped into a chair in my living room to text my friend again to explain my absence. And once again, exceedingly kindly, she came to my house. We called the doctor again, who insisted we summon an ambulance. I was no longer captain of my ship; indeed, my ship was listing, taking on water furiously, and just about to sink. I was, after the initial diagnosis, admitted to the hospital. Thus began my pilgrimage of suffering and healing, physical and spiritual growth.

When my friend said, "When all this is over," to what she referred was the result of a staphylococcus infection –not the dreaded Methicillin-resistant *Staphylococcus aureus* contracted in hospitals and requiring sterile treatments—but a virulent bacteria which, via some unknown access point, made its way into my system. Before it was done with me, I suffered a urinary-tract infection, swollen parotid glands which painfully puffed my face up like a pumpkin, a case of pneumonia, and, worst of all, nearly fatal sepsis. At the same time, the infection settled into my lower spine and psoas muscles on either side. Later, a physical therapist, looking at the reports of the seemingly countless magnetic resonance imaging scans I endured despite my claustrophobia, speculated that I might have slipped a disk during my exercising, which became a source of weakness in my body. She also suggested that since infections seek the weakest point to attack, an infected herniated lumbar disk could well have led to the spinal and adjacent muscular involvement. Later, both my highly respected neurosurgeon and the infectious-disease specialist accepted this premise as possible.

Eight days after my admission to the hospital, on the night of Friday the 13th, I had emergency and, as the neurosurgeon later said, exceedingly serious back surgery, deep and extensive, followed the next day by another procedure to excise the infection in the left psoas muscle. The right psoas muscle also showed signs of infection, but the recommendation, which I accepted, was that it was too small and deep to be safely excavated and also not ever likely to cause any trouble.

The afternoon of my initial surgery, two kind friends stayed with me until a couple hours before the 9:30 PM scheduled operation, and unbeknownst to me, both independently intended to return so that I would not be alone before the surgery. However, I was taken to the operating room sooner than anyone had expected, and we missed each other. Before they left, nevertheless, they had worried about whether I needed to see a priest that evening. One of them called the home number of a priest who had been to see me in the hospital. In an unfortunate bit of ill-timing, he was leaving for vacation the next day. Despite his burdens, he came and prayed with and for me. I told him that I was reminded of the beginning of Paul's letter to the Philippians (1:20–25 [NRSV]), where he says that he does not know whether it is better to die or to live. Dying means to go to be with Christ, but living means that there is still work to do. I felt I could leave this in God's hands. Of course, I had no alternative.

I remember the night after my surgery in the recovery room. It is a dim memory, but what I seem to recall is such excruciating pain that I thought I was on fire. It seems likely that I was screaming at the top of my lungs. Me, a fat, 60-something, old lady. A sensitive, caring nurse held me in her arms, expressing comforting and comfortable words. Sometime later, my bed and I were wheeled into my third hospital room. It was the only time during my hospitalization that I was attended by a male nurse. The gloomy space was unfamiliar; he was unknown, and while he did all that he was supposed to, he seemed alien, dispassionate, and disconnected from me. I do not mean to be sexist nor to disparage professionalism, but before and after that night I had many, many, many compassionate, considerate female nurses, who treated me both warmly and expertly. Still, that night, as I drifted in and out of consciousness, it seemed a personal Walpurgisnacht, an entranceway to hell, a very dark night of the soul.

The next morning my priest came to see me again before he left on vacation. He put his cell phone number in the memory of my mobile so I might call him if I needed to. What can I say? Agape. Also, my friends surrounded me. Simply put, I could not have managed on my own without the help of my friends, their presence and their prayers.

When he came to my room, the neurosurgeon informed me that the first operation had to be much deeper and broader than anticipated. He said, "Your body will consider this surgery, which was done in your best interests of course, as an assault, and your recovery will be more from the surgical aftereffects than from the infection." However, as my recovery played out, the disk pain also lingered for a long, long time.

In the hospital, I was in a dire predicament. I could not go to the bathroom by myself. In fact, I could not walk unassisted anywhere. Because of the Groshong catheter line in my chest in order best to deliver the antibiotics that my body needed to attack the staph infections, I could not take a bath or shower. I doubt that I smelled like a bed of flowers. Moreover, that circumstance, that catheter line, stayed with me for four months. Before I went home others even had to give me sponge baths because I could not do that myself. Frequently, I needed someone to adjust my pain medicine or something else for me. I often physically had to be lifted up for one thing or another, and I am no lightweight. While I was in the hospital I was helpless, dependent upon others for everything.

Yet, in the hospital, though I lacked the words even to think this at that time, I felt that in my illness God was all around me and did not expect me to recite formal, liturgical prayer in order for me to know he was with me. I was as mentally and emotionally ravaged and broken as I was physically. I asked friends to bring me a Book of Common Prayer (the Episcopal guide and mainstay) and a Bible. To my mortification (as I felt later), I could barely crack their spines. In the hospital, I could not pray the Daily Office (the set prayers and scriptural lectionary of the Church) nor my own personal diurnal devotions. Once or twice I read some psalms. What spoke to me was this: "For God alone my soul in silence waits" (Ps 62:1[BCP Psalter]). That much was surely true. I wanted to read and recite the written prayers but could not. Rather, what I felt, though at the time I had neither words nor even images, was that a divine presence filled those three different hospital rooms in which I had lain. It was an experience of Celtic thin space. Truly, I felt bathed and surrounded by God's healing love made manifest to me in those generous folks that took the time to visit me or send cards or flowers and pray for me. And I learned that a gift of living like that is to pray without ceasing (1 Thess 5:16 [NRSV]). In my illness, God was surely with me, all around me, and did not expect me to keep up with formal, liturgical prayer that I as a lifelong Episcopalian had been taught to use in order for me to know that he was with me. Perhaps, in truth, I needed my routine to be stopped and myself to be silenced in order truly to hear that "still, small voice"; "a soft, murmuring sound"; the "sound of sheer silence" (I Kings 19:12 [KJV, TANAKH, NRSV]). It was a kind of religious awakening for me, unlike any other experience I had ever had.

Months later, my spiritual director likened what I described to the next part of Paul's letter to the Philippians following what I have already cited, where the epistler includes an early hymn that states that Jesus "who, though he was in the form of God, did not regard equality with God as something to be exploited, but emptied himself, taking the form of a slave, being born in human likeness and being found in human form, he humbled himself and became obedient to the point of death—even death on a cross" (2:5–8 [NRSV]), the most profound model for believers of Christian living, becoming Christ-like. Christian mystics teach that we must learn to let go, to die to the world, so that we can be reborn in Christ. Like it or not, I was surely letting go. There was nothing else I could do.

In all, I stayed two weeks in the hospital; had two weeks in residential rehabilitation with daily physical and occupational therapies (OT, PT); and, then, eight or nine weeks at home receiving therapy. There, I had twice weekly OT and PT in separate sessions; weekly visits from a nurse to be sure that I remained alive and to check the maintenance of my 24-hour Groshong catheter, steadily delivering the antibiotic that I had, not easily, learned to change daily, all the while taking oral painkillers including, for many weeks, morphine and muscle relaxants. At the same time, I hobbled around my three-story house on a walker through June, July, and August. Fortunately, the PT at Rehab had had me practice using stairs. Once I was cleared to drive, I had two months of on-site PT, lugging my walker along in the back seat. I recall that I was still using the walker when I went to vote on Election Day in November.

Still, I hoped against hope to be independent again. Meanwhile, my sustaining good fortune meant, for two months, delivery thrice weekly of tasty dinners with lots of leftovers from unbelievably caring friends. One good friend and former nurse was willing to come to my house when I was first sent home to sort through all my medicine to determine the regimens. All summer long, other friends washed my clothes; shopped; took me to doctors' appointments, shopping, and church; visited; and took my seemingly abandoned car out for a spin, and a stalwart friend read out loud the term papers and final exams for which I had the foresight not to have graded before illness befell me. In the hospital, in rehab, and at home until I could be taken to church, others weekly brought me Holy Communion.

So what had I lost in those three months?

My preconceived notions of myself as an independent, self-sufficient agent

My resistance to the social and familial activities and life of my parish

My haughtiness and disdain in general toward the world from my assumed superior intellectual pedestal

Conceit, arrogance, solipsism, vanity, pride, lack of charity, and on and on and on.

I had been knocked down, run over, and opened up.

Hospitals are notoriously bright places. In that brightness and afterwards in rehab and at home, everything was made visible; all my faults were laid bare. What did I get instead of these vices, wrenched out of me by the enemies of good health? What I did know was this: "When evildoers came upon me to eat up my flesh, It was they, my foes and adversaries, who stumbled and fell" (Ps 27:2[BCP Psalter]); and "Look upon me and answer me,

O Lord my God, give light to my eyes, lest I sleep in death; Lest my enemies say, 'I have prevailed over him,' and my foes rejoice that I have fallen" (Psalm 13: 3–4[BCP Psalter]). Evildoers, adversaries, and foes felled me, but I also learned, early on, who held me up.

Now illuminated, new world opened before my eyes, epitomized by but by no means limited to a church community, radiating outward to friends, relatives, acquaintances of varying degrees of intimacy, all of whom rushed in to help me, to tend to me. People who continued to come to see me throughout the summer, sharing books they thought I would like and bringing fruit, meals, beverages, cat food, flowers, and most of all themselves brought me the wider, external world. As I have said, clergy and lay ministers brought Holy Communion every week, but I also discovered the communion of friends who came to spend time with me, to give of themselves to me. They surrounded me with such acceptance and love—acceptance, mind you, of me at my lowest, weakest, grubbiest, most bedraggled, least interesting and entertaining state—sheer, unadulterated, unprocessed, unpasteurized, pure and accepting love, God Love, agape, that I really cannot begin to count the ways that I have felt embraced, and for what? For nothing? I was the lowest of the low. I gave nothing. All I could offer was my insignificant gratitude. I had/have nothing to offer, to give. In the hospital, I had been entirely bedridden, helpless, unwashed. I was not much better in rehab or at home. My convalescence was (it seemed at the time) slow though forward-moving. I could not be who I had been. In truth, back then, I did not know who I had become. In the face of God, who was I?

Until my illness, I unquestioningly accepted the official doctrine of the church as how it defines itself. I had thought I knew very firmly, rigidly, implacably, what the church is. It is the body of Christ, I could avow and repeat the words of St. Paul: "For Christ is like a single body with its many limbs and organs, which, many as they are, together make up one body. For indeed we were all brought into one body by baptism. . ." (1Cor 12: 12–13 [REB]). I have taught Paul; I knew it all. What I believed was that the church is a formal, visible structure in the world. Of course, the most important part is not visible. However, that meant personal prayer; Eucharist; Morning Prayer, which I relentlessly, virtuously, and proudly attended every day; sacred music; sitting/standing/kneeling in proper Episcopal fashion with other similarly knowing and able communicants during each service. That is the church in the world, and the spiritual community of that, I was sure, which surrounded me. This is what I would have sworn I knew to be true, before I became sick.

I was not entirely wrong, obviously. God is ever present for me, maybe even more powerfully, in all those manifestations. But what I missed and what I gained in my lost months, lost time, is the true body of Christ. There are three things that last forever, says St. Paul, "faith, hope, and love" (1 Cor 13:13 [NRSV]), and I had long congratulated myself on my literal mastery of the first two and an intellectualized but not emotionally, profoundly felt—but surely my way was better—understanding of the third. But who knew? I was wrong about all three of them, as it turned out.

b. The Wilderness of My Lost Time

"At once the Spirit drove him out into the wilderness, and there he remained for forty days tempted by Satan. He was among the wild beasts; and the angels attended to his needs" (Mark 1:12–13 [REB]). The entirety of this experience from the onset of illness through my hospitalization and complete rehabilitation had in fact been a wilderness experience, a testing, a trial. I was beset by the beastly infections but ever waited upon by angelic friends.

Late in July, as the morphine was being diminished but the back pain persisted unrelentingly, I was switched to a milder painkiller, meloxicam. I did not realize and failed to look up on the Internet to learn that meloxicam is a nonsteroidal anti-inflammatory drug (NSAID). Several years before, I had been hospitalized when I could not walk because of extreme shortness of breath and chest pains, which led to a diagnosis of severe anemia, itself caused by NSAID-evoked gastric ulcers. I was cautioned never to take NSAIDs, so I assiduously avoided aspirin, Advil, Excedrin, Aleve, and their kinfolk. But I did not know about meloxicam.

Thus, in July, right after I was put on a pain medicine for the shooting nerve pains in my leg, I found myself unable to move because of extreme shortness of breath and chest pains. My earlier medical history did not occur to me; instead I was focused on my most recent medical story. So it was off to the emergency room once again, this time transported by a generous friend who stayed all day and into the night until I was placed in a room, to discover anemia redux and gastric ulceration. Once again, my priest came to see me. An amiable nursing technical assistant was attending me when he came by. My share of the double room was so small that we had stored my visitor's chair in the bathroom. When I sent the priest in there to retrieve it, the tech's eyes widened over the good-looking young visitor I had, and she whispered, "Is he your son?" The same friend who had brought me to the hospital later counseled that I should have replied, "No, he is my father."

My second hospitalization, though shorter than the first, had its own characteristics. Because I was still on the 24-hour, catheter-delivered antibiotic (which lasted into August), I had at times three intravenous lines simultaneously, the antibiotic, ulcer medication, and blood transfusions to the extent that ultimately amounted to a half gallon of blood. I am AB+, so my first transfusion was that, but then, as a universal recipient, I received the second most common type of blood (after O), for the second pint, A+. I was, disappointed, however, not to receive B+ as the third, which would have satisfied my desire for symmetry. But B+ is the second rarest form of blood, second only to AB. One cannot have everything one wants, as I was surely learning.

> "In the wilderness," as the psalter reviews,
> He led them with a cloud by day
> And all night long with a glow of fire.
> He split the hard rocks in the wilderness
> And gave them drink, as from the great deep. . . .
> He rained down manna upon them to eat and gave them
> the grain from heaven.
> (Ps 78:15, 14–24)

How often they rebelled against him in the wilderness;
and grieved him in the desert. . . (Psalm 78:40 [NRSV])

He led them through the deeps as through a wilderness.
He delivered them from the foe,
  redeemed them from the enemy. (TANAKH Ps 106:
9b–10)

. . . there in the desert they tried God's patience.
He gave them what they asked
but followed it with a wasting sickness. (Ps 106: 14b–15)

I have come to see my hospitalizations, rehabilitation, and convalescence at home as a time of wilderness, wandering in the desert, the darkness of dry awareness, and yet where I was not ever truly alone.

For one thing, I rarely had a single day without a visitor in the summer, who brought meals, gifts, groceries, things I had requested. Accordingly, like the Israelites in the desert who received manna and quail and water from rocks for sustenance and the cloud and the pillar of fire for guidance, I was nurtured and led, and no doubt tutored and taught, by my friends, by God. I am coming to the awareness and hard-won acknowledgment that I am, like us all, a child of God (not the mature intellectual self I fancied). It is astounding to me how much I keep learning, that all these benevolent people who gave of themselves, their time, their interest, and their resources were and are agents of God, angels of God, acting as vehicles of the divine. It had been a summer of hell, as many who commiserated suggested.

On one hand, nonetheless, considering hell, I have reflected that that suggests punishment. No, neither hospitalization, I believe, was punitive. Was I in hell? Perhaps. Yet I never felt far from God and his kingdom, and hell is separation from God, I have heard, from some who know, I guess. In some ways, I felt closer than I had ever been to the divine. I do not mean to be a martyr or, heaven knows, to be self-serving, so I need to look at my experience objectively and intellectually. One might say—rather than bemoaning, bewailing, O, Lord, why me; why not someone else? — I

can see one novel way of looking at my experience. All that happened was not because I needed some kind of punishment, but,
in the grand scheme of things, one might add up such factors as
that I have good health insurance, had inexplicably made no plans
for the summer, had just retired, have no commitments to other
people; there was no one, therefore, that I let down by getting sick.
Rather, among God's children, I was someone who could weather
these challenges. In the spinning of the cosmic wheel of fortune,
if I were to subscribe to that, if all this had to happen to someone,
it could not have happened to a nicer person, yes? My spiritual
director reminds me of the Ignatian conceit of consolation without
cause for I did nothing to bring on my illness, as a smoker's actions
might lead to lung cancer or a misstep and a fall might lead to a
broken bone. Instead, the question is not why me, why did this
misfortune befall poor old me, but, more to the point, why was
conceited, selfish, arrogant, uncharitable I given God's grace?

Ultimately, it seemed, long-term convalescence is like being on a diet. There are plateaus, immediate improvements, slow
improvements, stases, seeming backsliding, and regression. It is a
long journey, and whither it turns is not in my hands. It is not all
about me. In the hospital the first time, as I have said, I could not
pray in words, yet I was praying without ceasing, lying in God's
arms of love. In the second hospitalization and before and after
it, at home, I could pray formally as had been my style, but now
informally, even wordlessly.

Once again, the second time in the hospital, caring friends
brought me a Bible and a Book of Common Prayer so that I could
read the Daily Office with appropriate scriptural passages. So was
I in hell? Or heaven? No, I am not that much of a martyr. Yes,
indeed, it was a hell of a summer. But the outpouring of love and
kindness made it a taste of paradise, a gift of grace that I had nothing with which to do, that I had done nothing to earn. Yet I was
given the opportunity to be reborn, to be baptized anew, to find
the community that is the true Body of Christ in the Trinity and
the communion of saints, what Wordsworth in Book X of his mag-
isterial autobiographical poem *The Prelude* (1805) figured as "One

great Society alone on earth/ the noble Living and the noble Dead"
(lines 968–969) where the mystery of our spiritual life in Christ is
to be emptied before him, and we learn to give our lives to him and
to his service. Who am I in the face of God? I must learn to be fully
formed into the person God wants me to be, which is to what this
new baptism must lead.

c. What I Gained

I must ponder the meaning of the word *gratitude*. How can I express my gratitude? I live in a state of gratitude, to my friends, to
God, to numerous people to whom I am indebted. My experiences
bestowed three lessons about how to express gratitude.

First, later, when I worried how I could ever repay all these
people, my priest hushed me when I brought that matter up to
him. "People want to help you, Laura. If you try to repay, you are
making a commercial transaction out of their goodness. You are
demeaning what they have done." In other words, do not worry
about reciprocity. Instead, worry about those who need your attention right now. Pay it forward.

Second, my friend from back in the day when I went to
Morning Prayer who had stood by and assisted through all my
ordeal told me how that experience of sharing the Morning Prayer
liturgy had made her feel, those four of us regulars, a part of our
parish community, which disintegrated when my continued absence coincided with the departures of one who moved away and
another who changed churches. But by being among the legion
that did immeasurable good for me, those innumerable tasks, she
felt again within the community and family of the Church.

Third, later on, there were all those people who thanked me
for allowing them to do things for me. Imagine that, as if I were
the means rather than the beneficiary. These are three ways to consider gratitude.

All this has made me think about thanksgiving. For the
formal, established church, the Eucharist means thanksgiving. In
my faith tradition, it is a ceremonial, liturgical ritual that gives us

heavenly sustenance, brings us to share with the apostles in Christ's sacrifice, for which we should be, are to be, and are grateful. We are grateful that Christ sacrifices himself for us. I am also learning to be grateful for the gifts of time and talents given of themselves, from my friends, from those who brought Christ to me in the Holy Communion. Other friends have brought Christ to me in their acts of exemplary, many-faceted generosity. I am immersed in gratitude for that and for them. Their kindness marks them as genuine agents and children of God. I am grateful constantly as I am also learning to pray without ceasing, ever to be mindful of the presence of God in my life, as Henri Nouwen defines that passage from Thessalonians. My prayer, while wordless, is a prayer of Thanksgiving. Truly I could not have endured those months of suffering and recovery without my friends. A friend is one who makes sacrifices. I am learning how to be grateful in prayer, in life, in living.

People have said to me, "How many friends you have." Yes, I do. What I respond, the truth with which I tamp down my inner pridefulness, is to say, "Agape." It is the goodness and kindness of people around me, in the community of my parish of St. James', of the Episcopal Church at large, of the Christian Church universal and farther because many more than just Episcopalians helped me. That was a gift to me to learn. Their kindness had nothing to do with me. I was just the lucky target, at the wrong place at the wrong time, which made it all right, made it, in fact, gifts of grace.

The time I am describing advances a lesson I had many years ago but had not fully appreciated or implemented.

When I was twenty-three years old, full of myself, about to earn a Master of Arts in English from Bryn Mawr, I decided to leave graduate school for a while to work in the real world. Consequently, I rented a tiny, third-floor, walk-up studio apartment in Center City Philadelphia and secured a job as a proofreader for what was then the largest public accounting firm in Pennsylvania. As far as public accountants were concerned at least in those days, proofreading English majors were at the extreme bottom of the corporate ladder, perhaps even below the lowest rung. I earned a tiny, tiny income though I was paid time and half for overtime during tax season. I swiftly learned that all the other proofreaders had high-school diplomas, period. That was all that the job required. I did not need my summa cum laude BA, junior year Phi Beta Kappa, or the imminent MA. All I needed to do was to be kind and be interested in other people, to meet them where they were, to learn to love them as they were, not as I thought they ought to be. How else could I get along? We spent long, tedious hours, from 7:45 AM to 5:15 PM, with a 15-minute coffee break in the morning and a 45-minute lunch, in two-person cubicles, reading columns of numbers aloud to each other. Dreariness, absolute tedium. Despite my English degree, the only punctuation marks that mattered were the commas and periods used in numerals. Finally, to add insult to injury, we had to check all the arithmetic on adding machines. (This was in 1976, pre-computer.) In that environment, it did not pay to be a shrew or a snob. This was Chapter One.

Chapter Two of that experience came in the hospital. During my crises and convalescences, the nurses and techs in the hospital and at rehab repeatedly told me I was their favorite patient. I could not imagine why. These caring souls came into my room, these hardworking caretakers of me, marveling at my number of visitors and saying, "But you never complain." "You never whine." "You do not blame us for your sickness or discomfort." "You always say 'please' and 'thank you,' even when we take blood for tests." What can I say? I want to live in a civil, respectful world. The most important rule, notwithstanding who you are, what degrees you have, how much money you make, what your gifts are, or what your needs might be, is always to be kind and loving, in order to bring the kingdom of God here among us. Yes, as I learned, I have much work yet to do.

The gospel for the Third Sunday of Advent, the middle of December, seven months after May, includes the lines, "'Go and tell John what you hear and see: the blind receive their sight; the lame walk, the lepers are cleansed, the deaf hear, the dead are raised . . .'"(Matt 11:4 [NRSV]). I listened to this passage read out loud by the deacon that Sunday, and when it came time for Communion,

I took a deep breath, put down my cane, and walked unassisted to the altar rail. There, for the first time since Sunday, May 1, I knelt to receive the Body and Blood of our Lord. It was a couple years later till I could put the cane down for good, but in that moment in the strength of the Body of Christ of the Church, I felt securely lifted up. As the prophet says, ". . . He makes me sure-footed as a hind and sets my feet on the heights" (Hab 3:19 [REB]).

In the fall, I went to see my internist who said, "You've certainly had an eventful year." I spared you, my patient reader, the slipped-disk/pinched-nerve-in-my-neck-in-January yarn, which began 2016 before all the events from May onward unrolled which I have just recounted. Such is life. Throughout all this, I truly was blessed with wonderful medical care, compassionate and knowledgeable physicians and nurses, especially an infectious-disease specialist who would not give up on me, even when everyone else at the hospital that first week felt there was nothing more that could be done, who called me "Dr. Dabundo" when I was discharged the first time and chose to be the one from her practice to see me when she espied my name for the second hospitalization, along with the well-established neurosurgeon who performed emergency major surgery on me late one Friday night. Additionally, I cannot say that I was not made better without prayer. "Weeping may spend the night, but joy comes in the morning" (Ps. 30:6 [BCP Psalter]). My spiritual director reminds me that the word *salvation* comes from the root of the word *healing*. I have been physically healed; the spiritual journey toward salvation has just begun, toward a place and a moment when the parallel converge.

Bibliography

Baum, L. Frank. *The Wonderful Wizard of Oz*. New York: Dover, 1996.

The Bible, the Authorized King James Version. New York: Oxford University Press, 1997.

Blake, William. *The Poetry and Prose of William Blake*. Edited by David V. Erdman. Garden City, NY: Doubleday, 1970.

The Book of Common Prayer and Administration of the Sacraments and Other Rites and Ceremonies of the Church According to the Use of the Protestant Episcopal Church in the United States of America Together with The Psalter or Psalms of David. New York: The Church Pension Fund, 1945.

The Book of Common Prayer and Administration of the Sacraments and Other Rites and Ceremonies of the Church Together with The Psalter or Psalms of David, in *Prayer Book and Hymnal*. New York: Church Publishing Company, 2006.

Brandeis, Madeline. *Little Anne of Canada*. The Children of All Lands Stories. New York: Grosset & Dunlap, 1931.

————. *The Little Dutch Tulip Girl*. New York: Grosset & Dunlap, 1929.

————. *Shaun O'Day of Ireland*. New York: Grosset & Dunlap, 1931.

Buber, Martin. *I and Thou*. Translated by Walter Kaufmann. New York: Charles Scribner's Sons, 1970.

Capote, Truman. *In Cold Blood*. New York: Signet, 1967.

Carroll, Lewis. *The Annotated Alice: Alice's Adventures in Wonderland & Through the Looking Glass*. 83–91. New York: Clarkson N. Potter, 1960.

Davies, Oliver, and Fiona Bowie, eds. *Celtic Christian Spirituality: An Anthology of Medieval and Modern Sources*. New York: Continuum, 1997.

Davies, Oliver, translator. *Celtic Spirituality*. New York: Paulist, 1999.

De Quincey, Thomas. *Confessions of an English Opium Eater*. New York: Penguin, 1986.

De Waal, Esther. *The Celtic Way of Prayer: The Recovery of the Religious Imagination*. New York: Doubleday, 1997.

————. *Every Earthly Blessing; Rediscovering the Celtic Tradition*. Harrisburg, PA: Morehouse, 1999.

Driscoll, Herbert. *The Road to Donaguile: A Celtic Spiritual Journey.* New York: Cowley, 2000.

Eliot, T. S. *Four Quartets.* Boston: Mariner, 1968.

Frye, Northrop. *The Great Code: The Bible and Literature.* New York: Harcourt Brace Jovanovich, 1981.

The Holy Bible containing the Old and New Testaments with the Apocryphal/Deuterocanonical Books, New Revised Standard Version. New York: Oxford University Press, 1989.

The Hymnal 1982, in *Prayer Book and Hymnal.* New York: Church Publishing Company, 2006.

Jeschonek, Robert. *Penn Traffic Forever.* n.p.: First Pie, 2015.

Joyce, Timothy. *Celtic Christianity: A Sacred Tradition, a Vision of Hope.* Maryknoll, NY: Orbis Books, 1999.

Lao Tzu and Stephen Mitchell. *Tao Te Ching: A New English Version.* New York: Harper, 2006.

McCullough, David. *The Johnstown Flood.* New York: Simon and Schuster, 1987.

Newell, J. Philip. *The Book of Creation: An Introduction to Celtic Spirituality.* New York, Paulist, 1999.

———. *Christ of the Celts: The Healing of Creation.* San Francisco: Jossey Bass, 2008.

———. *Listening for the Heartbeat of God. A Celtic Spirituality.* Paulist, 1997.

Nouwen, Henri. J. M. "Unceasing Prayer." In *Spiritual Direction; Wisdom for the Long Walk of Faith.* 56-60. New York: HarperOne, 2015.

O'Connor, Flannery. "A Good Man is Hard to Find." In *Three: Wise Blood, A Good Man Is Hard to Find, The Violent Bear It Away,* 129–143. New York: Farrar, Straus and Giroux, 1971.

O'Donohue, John. *Anam Cara: A Book of Celtic Wisdom.* New York: HarperCollins, 1998.

Reich, Charles. *The Greening of America.* New York: Bantam, 1972.

The Revised English Bible with the Apocrypha. n.p.: Oxford University Press and Cambridge University Press, 1989.

Roker, Al. *Ruthless Tide: The Heroes and Villains of the Johnstown Flood: America's Astonishing Gilded Age Disaster.* New York: William Morrow, 2019.

Sellner, Edward C. *The Celtic Soul Friend: A Trusted Guide for Today.* Notre Dame, IN: Ave Maria, 2002.

———. *Stories of the Celtic Soul Friends: Their Meaning for Today.* New York: Paulist, 2004.

Sewell, Anna. *Black Beauty.* New York: Sterling, 2004.

Simpson, Ray. *Exploring Celtic Spirituality: Historic Roots for Our Future.* Columbia, MO: Kingsgate, 2004.

Starhawk. *The Spiral Dance: A Rebirth of the Ancient Religion of the Great Goddess.* San Francisco: Harper & Row, 1979.

Suzuki, D. T. *Zen Buddhism: Selected Writings of D. T. Suzuki*. Edited by William Barrett. New York: Doubleday Anchor, 1956.

TANAKH, A New Translation of The Holy Scriptures According to the Traditional Hebrew Text. Philadelphia: The Jewish Publication Society, 1985.

Wordsworth, William. William Wordsworth. The Oxford Authors. Edited by Stephen Gill. New York: Oxford University Press, 1990.

Made in the USA
Columbia, SC
26 September 2021

46217875R00075